ARKANA

The Shaman and the Magician

Nevill Drury was educated in England and Australia where he now lives. He has a master's degree in anthropology and has written or co-authored thirty books, including *Don Juan, Mescalito and Modern Magic* and *Inner Visions*, both published by Arkana, and *The Occult Sourcebook*. He has appeared on numerous television and radio programmes dealing with the potential of human consciousness and has given lectures and workshops at a number of major conferences. He divides his time between publishing, editing and writing.

The Shaman and the Magician

JOURNEYS BETWEEN THE WORLDS

Nevill Drury

ARKANA

ARKANA

Published by the Penguin Group
Penguin Books Ltd, 80 Strand, London WC2R 0RL, England
Penguin Putnam Inc., 375 Hudson Street, New York, New York 10014, USA
Penguin Books Australia Ltd, 250 Camberwell Road, Camberwell, Victoria 3124, Australia
Penguin Books Canada Ltd, 10 Alcorn Avenue, Toronto, Ontario, Canada M4V 3B2
Penguin Books India (P) Ltd, 11 Community Centre, Panchsheel Park, New Delhi – 110 017, India
Penguin Books (NZ) Ltd, Cnr Rosedale and Airborne Roads, Albany, Auckland, New Zealand
Penguin Books (South Africa) (Pty) Ltd, 24 Sturdee Avenue, Rosebank 2196, South Africa

Penguin Books Ltd, Registered Offices: 80 Strand, London WC2R 0RL, England

www.penguin.com

First published by Routledge & Kegan Paul Ltd 1982
Published by Arkana 1987
3

Copyright © Nevill Drury, 1982
All rights reserved

Printed in England by Clays Ltd, St Ives plc

For Susan, Rebecca and Megan

Contents

Illustrations

Foreword

I first met Nevill Drury at an international conference on Phillip Island in Australia in November of 1980. From his works, I already respected him as a sophisticated and prolific author, and expected to meet a man in at least late middle age. Much to my surprise, Nevill turned out to be only in his early thirties. In retrospect, perhaps I should have guessed as much from his books, for in them he is characteristically concerned with questions of consciousness, visionary experience, and the occult that are a legacy of the psychedelic sixties. Like many others of his generation, he found the works of Carlos Castaneda and the literature on shamanism and occultism relevant to the search for answers to these question. Indeed, one of Nevill Drury's books, 'Don Juan, Mescalito, and Modern Magic', addressed itself specifically to resemblances between the world-view of Castaneda's shaman, don Juan, and that of late nineteenth-and twentieth-century Western practitioners of occult magic.

In the present book Nevill Drury continues his search for common denominators between shamanism and contemporary western occultism. In this exploration he brings to bear approximately a decade and a half of practical experience working within the framework of occult western magic and combines the experience with an anthropological knowledge of shamanism. The results are extremely interesting. Nevill Drury demonstrates, perhaps better than anyone has ever done before, that modern western occult magic sometimes has trance and visionary aspects that are unexpectedly similar to those of classic shamanism. By drawing on a thorough knowledge of a literature that is often as obscure as it is occult, he makes a strong case for the shamanic parallels of some of the modern magical cult practices. The 'rising in the planes' and 'path-workings' of the twentieth-century visionary magician, for example, are clearly partial analogues of the shaman's journey to the upper world and lower world. But there are also differences, as when the magician utilises Tarot archetypes, adopts ancient Egyptian or Dianic cosmology, or follows a leader's recitation into guided fantasy. Still, the similarities are greater than many would expect, and one wonders if the Inquisition did not do as thorough a job in eradicating 'witchcraft' (shamanism) from Europe as is commonly assumed. While it is true that the psychedelic ointments of late medieval and Renaissance times are not today part of western occult magic, it does seem likely that there was a slender thread of continutiy as represented, for example, by some of the practices of the Hermetic Order of the Golden Dawn at the turn of the century. Of course, it is possible that the parallels between shamanism and western occult magic are mainly due to a rediscovery, through trial and error, of 'what works'. Whatever the ultimate reasons for the interesting similarities pointed out here by Nevill Drury, he has made a rare and fascinating contribution by bringing them to light.

Michael Harner
New York City
12 February 1981

Preface and Acknowledgments

There has been a revival of interest in the elusive figure of the shaman, who is both the medicine man and magician, the mystic and healer. The anthropological literature on shamanism is extensive and such scholars as Mircea Eliade, Michael Harner, Peter Furst, Erika Bourguignon, Agehananda Bharati, Joan Halifax, and A. F. Anisimov, among others, have made notable contributions to the subject. However, popular interest in the role of the shaman and his contribution to modern thought has undoubtedly been heightened by the international success of the works of Carlos Castaneda whose encounters with the shaman-sorcerer don Juan have become legendary.

With some justification, Richard de Mille has highlighted inconsistencies of an anthropological and linguistic nature in the Castaneda writings and these have been included in de Mille's own works 'Castaneda's Journey' and 'The Don Juan Papers'. However, the fact remains that whether Castaneda's shamanic accounts are totally authentic or include fictional components, the essential themes and world-view presented remain consistent with the shamanic perspective. It is possible to speak of shamanism as a universal mode linking man with the cosmos by means of the magical journey since, as anthropologists have discovered, the essential themes of shamanism are remarkably similar whether in Siberia, Japan, Australia or the Americas.

My interest in this material is twofold. My academic training is in anthropology but my personal spiritual orientation, if one can modestly call it that, is towards the western mystery tradition. Accordingly, the great themes which shamanism and western magic have in common have not been brought together here merely as an academic exercise, but to show that even in a modern urban context the mythic approaches to human consciousness continue to play a vital role alongside scientific technology.

We are talking essentially, of the possible alternative that the western mystery tradition of magic and mythology offers to the person who is not able physically to embark on a shamanic journey with a Jivaro or Huichol Indian. Since this book is intended for the general reader interested in shamanic and magical thought, I have isolated a more analytical chapter on states of consciousness as Appendix A. Such psychological perspectives are of academic interest but to some extent conflict with the essential poetry of shamanism and visionary magic which I hope will be apparent from the mythic journeys described in this book.

I would like to thank the following people for kindly allowing me to reproduce copyright material: Dolores Ashcroft-Nowicki for passages from 'Highways of the Mind', first published in 'Round Merlin's Table'; Catherine Colefax and Cheryl Weeks for the 'entry' and 'magical journey' to the Cosmic Dragon; Moses Aaron for his account of the magical encounter with Pan.

The Shaman and the Magician

1   *A Jivaro shaman photographed by Michael Harner*

CHAPTER 1
The World of the Shaman

In 1951 a legendary Iban healer named Manang Bungai performed a dramatic ritual which was believed to slay an incubus, or evil spirit, that had been blamed for the death of a seven-month-old baby girl.

Bungai, clad in a loin cloth and carrying a spear, entered a darkened room and began summoning the incubus by means of various invocations and also by tempting it with food. His audience was unable to clearly perceive what was happening and was in a state of heightened suggestibility.

Very soon there was a yelping sound and a noisy scuffle, after which Bungai emerged with a blood smeared spear claiming he had inflicted mortal wounds on the incubus. Several experienced Iban hunters were aware that Bungai had in fact been doing battle with a monkey and the anthropologist observing the event, Derek Freeman, was later able to verify this by means of blood tests. However the majority of the Iban present at the ceremony believed that their healing magician was engaged in a mystical encounter.

The case of Bungai represents the shaman-who-is-not. True shamanism is characterised by access to other realms of consciousness. As Mircea Eliade notes: 'the shaman specializes in a trance during which his soul is believed to leave his body and ascend to the sky or descend to the underworld.'[1]

Indeed, the shaman is a master of spirit entities, a venturer on different cosmic planes. When the would-be Jivaro shaman ventures near the sacred waterfalls to seek the power of the *arutam wakan*, the soul force identified with the visionary experience, he takes *natema*, a hallucinogenic beverage made from the Banisteriopsis vine, which allows access to the spirit world. In his visions he may see rolling towards him a pair of giant mythic jaguars fighting viciously or alternatively two enormous writhing snakes, and it is his task to master the reality of the vision by running forward to touch it. Anthropologist Michael Harner who, himself experienced psychedelic initiation with the Indians, notes that for the Jivaro the supernatural is the real world, and in this sense confirms the idea of the shaman as a 'master of ecstasy'. But the shaman is also in a very real sense a 'traveller', a visionary who has access to other dimensions of experience.

The remarkable case of Deguchi Onisaburo is one of the most extraordinary examples of this type of shamanism and gave rise to the Omoto religious movement in Japan.

In 1898, Deguchi, who was by all accounts a frail youth, was beaten up by some gamblers and nearly died. A short while later he sank into a comatose sleep and on recovering consciousness declared that he had journeyed to a cave on Mt Takakuma and after fasting there had travelled through regions of Heaven and Hell. On his journey he had been granted occult powers such as clairvoyance and clairaudience and had seen back as far as the creation of the world. His visionary experiences included a meeting with the king of the underworld who in a moment was able to transform from a white-haired old man with a gentle face into a frightening demonic monarch with a bright red face, eyes like mirrors and a tongue of flame.[2]

Embodying a theme which recurs in shamanism – the transformation of the symbolic vision – we see from the account that time and again Deguchi is 'killed, split in half with a sharp blade like a pear, dashed to pieces on rocks, frozen, burnt, engulfed in avalanches of snow . . . turned into a goddess' and yet he still emerges from his journey victorious over the forces of apparent death. It is this power which gives the shaman his awesome standing among his fellows. It is his conquest of the dangers and pitfalls of the visionary journey, even through death and rebirth, that places the shaman among 'the elect'. The themes of dismemberment, ascent to the sky, descent to the underworld are clearly initiatory.

It is significant, then, that after his ordeal Deguchi eventually finds himself at the centre of the world, at the summit of the huge axial mountain, Sumeru. He is granted a vision of the creation of the world and then comes to a river beyond which lies paradise. Before him and standing on a vast lotus he finds a marvellous palace of gold, agate and jewels. All around him are blue mountains and the golden lapping waves of a lake. Golden doves fly above him in the air.[3]

Several aspects of Deguchi's journey are typical of shamanism in general. He is in a state of psychic dissociation caused by his near death; he gains visionary powers from the beings he encounters; he journeys upon a magic mountain, which in other cultures equates in significance with the Cosmic Tree, and eventually arrives at the 'centre of the world'; his enlightenment includes a vision of the world's origin; vistas of serene and majestic landscapes, and imposing temples. Despite Deguchi's traumatic encounters with powerful cosmic forces he is finally a transformed and 'reborn' figure. Initiation is central to shamanism in the same way that it is a vital component of modern magic, and specific initiations tend to arise as crises at different stages of the mythic journey. From culture to culture these patterns of transformation take different forms according to the way in which the mythic universe is perceived and the nature of the hierarchies of gods who dwell there.

THE COSMOS AND ITS DENIZENS

In the sense that the shaman acts as an intermediary between the sacred and profane worlds, between mankind and the realm of gods and spirits, he has special access to a defined cosmos. The actual cosmology, in terms of levels and hierarchies may be reasonably basic, as it is with the Australian Aborigines and many South and Central American tribes, or it may be complex and highly structured, as in the case of Siberian shamanism.

For example the Jivaro believe that all knowledge pertaining to *tsentsak*, or magical power, derives from the mythical first shaman, Tsuni, who is still alive today. He lives underwater in a house whose walls are formed like palm staves by upright anacondas and sits on a turtle, using it as a stool. He is said to be white skinned with long hair and he supplies privileged shamans with special quartz crystals (*tsentsak*) which are particularly deadly. No shamans are able to stand up to or overcome Tsuni.[4]

The sky god of the Wiradjeri medicine men of Western New South Wales has a comparable function. Known as Baiame, he is described as a 'very great old man, with a long beard, sitting in his camp with his legs under him. Two great quartz crystals extend from his shoulders to the sky above him.'[5]

Baiame sometimes appears to the Aborigines in their dreams. He causes a sacred waterfall of liquid quartz to pour over their bodies absorbing them totally. They then grow wings replacing their arms. Later the dreamer learns to fly and Baiame sinks a piece of magical quartz into his forehead to enable him to see inside physical objects. Subsequently an inner flame and a heavenly cord are also incorporated into the body of the new shaman.[6]

The Mazatec Indians of Mexico, meanwhile, have been exposed to Christian influence and such elements have entered their cosmology while the indigenous component remains. The Mazatecs make use of psilocybe mushrooms and the female shamans use this altered state of consciousness to determine the causes of sickness. On a local level they believe that the groves and abysses are inhabited by the little people or dwarves known as the *laa*, but they have also assimilated into their belief systems Jesus Christ and the Virgin Mary.

Among the Mazatecs both the patient and the shaman take the sacred mushrooms, so that the sick person may hear the healing words which come from the spirit world and thereby share in the cure. Munn reports that as the shaman sinks deeper into trance she seems to go on a journey. She mutters: 'Let us go searching for the path, the tracks of her feet, the tracks of her nails. From the right side to the left side, let us look.' After several hours she appears to reach a peak:

There is the flesh of God, There is the flesh of Jesus Christ.
There with the Virgin.[7]

But if such shamanic pronouncements seem reasonably
orthodox they may often be infused with magic. Another
Mazatec ceremony includes the following:

> The aurora of the dawn is coming and the light of day. In
> the name of the Father, the Son and the Holy Spirit, by
> the sign of the Holy Cross, free us Our Lord from our
> enemies and all evil. . . .
> I am he who cures. I am he who speaks with the Lord
> of the World. I am happy. I speak with the mountains of
> peaks. I am he who speaks with Bald Mountain. I am the
> remedy and the medicine man, I am the mushroom. I am
> the fresh mushroom. I am the large mushroom. I am the
> fragrant mushroom. I am the mushroom of the spirit.[8]

Invariably the shamanic process entails direct contact and
rapport with the gods and goddesses who provide their followers
with first principles, with a sense of causality, balance, order
and with it health and well-being.

Especially among American Indians, for example the Desana
group of the Eastern Colombian Tukano, we find a strong
identification of the shaman's vision with the primal reality of
the cosmos:

> On awakening from the trance, the individual remains
> convinced of the religious teachings. He has seen every-
> thing; he has seen Vai-mahse, master of the Game animals,
> and the daughter of the Sun, he has heard her voice; he
> has seen the Snake canoe float out through the rivers and
> he has seen the first men spring from it.[9]

The concept of a system of rivers or an ocean of being from
which the Universe derives is also a common mythological
element in several unconnected cosmologies in both simple and
complex religions. Quite aside from shamanic accounts the idea
also occurs, for example, in the creation myths of the Babylon-
ians and in the Jewish Qabalistic mystery teachings.

Among the Evenks of Siberia the Universe is thought to have been born from a watery waste. Rivers feature predominantly in Evenk mythology and the shaman's helper spirits are often water birds like the duck or goldeneye.[10] The Evenk universe is a characteristically shamanic one in the sense that it conforms to the normal Siberian pattern of being divided into three worlds, upper, middle and lower, vertically aligned around a central axis or World Tree. The Evenk lives in the middle world. His options are upwards towards the benevolent sky dwellers, or downwards to the world of the dead, the spirit ancestors and the mistress of the Underworld. This dualism is reinforced by the fact that the term for the upper world (*uga buga*) has a linguistic origin in a phrase meaning 'toward morning' while that of the lower world (*khergu-ergu buga*) means 'towards night'.[11]

The Evenks believe the sky dwellers in *ugu buga* live a life comparable to that found in the middle world except on a more exalted level. For example Amaka, who taught the first Evenks how to use fire and make tools, is thought to be a very old man, dressed in fur clothing and living among treasures, gold, copper and silver. Around him are large herds grazing in lush pastures.[12] Other prominent Evenk deities include Eksheri, supreme master of animals, birds and fish and ruler of fate. Local spirit rulers of the hills, rivers and streams are subservient to him. He labours on behalf of the Evenks gathering heat for them and as Spring comes, his sons carry his bag and shake out the heat upon the middle world.

Khergu-ergu buga, on the other hand, represents a world which is quite the reverse of man's. Living things become dead there, and the dead come alive.[13] Animals and beings which were resident in the lower world become invisible if they transfer to the middle plane and accordingly shaman heroes who venture down into the underworld will be seen only by the shamans of that region.

In the Evenk underworld dwell deceased kinsmen and the spirits of evil and illness. The deceased continue to lay their traps there, and to fish and hunt, but their bodies are cold and lack the life essence of the middle world. Meanwhile the ancestor spirits who reside there are only half-human and are linked with totemic reincarnations. The possibility of a transfer of plane does exist however, and this is the shaman's role. The hole which leads into the heavenly vault is guarded by an old woman – the Mistress of the Universe – and she is sometimes visualised in an animal/human transformation with horns on her head. Her task at the entrance to heaven is to point the way to the dwelling of the ruler of the heavenly lights.

A similar female deity also guards the animals of the clan lands below the earth. In order to ensure a satisfactory hunt, the shaman journeys down below the roots of the sacred tree to visit her. Aided by spirit guides who help him overcome various obstacles which impede his path, he encounters the Clan Mistress and begs her to release animals for the hunt. She may be witholding animals from the middle world because vital taboos have been breached. The shaman seeks to capture from her magical threads which he hides in his special drum. When he returns to the middle world, he shakes these forth from his drum indicating that these threads will in turn transform into real animals.[14]

The symbolic Tree is a vital pillar in the cosmology for it connects the three planes of reality. The crown of the Tree reaches into the heavens, the trunk sustains the middle world and the roots extend down into the underworld. The shaman's drum is often made from the wood of the Cosmic Tree and thus symbolises his journey upon it. The Chumikan and Upper Zeya Evenks specifically identify the Tree with the source of life: 'Man was born from a tree. There was a tree, it split in two. Two people came out. One was a man, the other a woman.'[15] Mircea Eliade, meanwhile, identifies the Tree as a major motif within shamanism. 'The central practice', he writes, 'is to climb the axis of the world on an ecstatic journey to the Centre.'[16] In this sense the Centre is the cause of all being, the origin and source of explanation for all that happens in the waking world. It is interesting that both the mistress of heaven and the clan mistress of the underworld resemble each other except with dualistic connotations, so that what is above and below are also, so to speak, twin sides of the coin.

While several anthropologists have sought to identify shamanism with hunting practices, Eliade notes that the essential nature of the shamanic cosmology is much more broadly based:

> Although the shamanic experience proper could be evaluated as a mystical experience by virtue of the cosmological concept of the three communicating zones, this cosmological concept does not belong exclusively to the ideology of Siberian and Central Asian shamanism, nor in fact to any other shamanism. It is an universally disseminated idea connected with the belief in the possibility of direct communication with the sky. The shaman transforms a cosmo-theological concept into a concrete mystical experience . . . only for the shaman is real communication among the three cosmic zones a possibility.[17]

SYMBOLIC REGALIA AND EQUIPMENT

Since the shaman's role is to travel from one cosmic zone to another, it is not surprising that his entire function as a technician of the sacred should reflect the nature of the gods with whom he is dealing. The shaman characteristically seeks to act in a manner which is appropriate to the domain he is entering. Although he is often accompanied by animal-spirit guides, the shaman may, for example, transform into an animal on his journey. The Japanese shamans observed by Carmen Blacker characteristically wore a cap of eagle and owl feathers, their cloaks adorned with stuffed snakes. These 'all resolve into means whereby passage from one world to another is facilitated', 'the magic clothes and instruments, of which the drum is the most important, embody in their shape, in the materials of which they are made, in the patterns and figures engraved upon them, symbolic links with the other world.'[18]

Eliade similarly notes that by donning sacred costumes the shaman transcends profane space and prepares to enter into the sacred world.[19] The Yakut shaman wears a Kaftan that bears a solar disc, which is sometimes thought to be the opening through the earth which the shaman uses to enter the underworld. The coat of a Goldi shaman, meanwhile, bears motifs of the Cosmic Tree and animals like bears and leopards as well as a central Sun. Other costumes similarly reflect the prevailing mythology. The Buryat costume is heavily laden with iron ornaments which symbolise the iron bones of immortality while the bears and leopards, serpents and lizards which appear on it are the shaman's helping spirits.[20]

That the shaman should seek to identify strongly with the spirit realm is to be expected. His altered state of consciousness entails a transfer of awareness to a dimension where the ancestral myths become experiential realities in trance. The shaman's costume links him with the gods and identifies him as belonging with them as an appropriate intermediary.

The shaman's drum deserves special mention. On a physical level, its rim is invariably made of wood from the world tree – the larch among the Evenks for example – and its skin is directly linked with the animal the shaman rides into the underworld. The anthropologist Potapov discovered that among the Al Itai the shaman's drum derives its name not from the animals whose skins are used in the manufacture (like the camel or dappled horse) but the domestic animals ridden by the shaman in the middle world. In many shamanic cultures the drum *is* the steed and the monotonous rhythm which emanates from it is suggestive of the galloping of a horse on a journey.

On a contemplative level the sound of the drum thus acts as a focusing device for the shaman. It creates an atmosphere of concentration and resolve, enabling him to sink deep into trance as he shifts his attention to the inner journey of the spirit. Erika Bourguignon notes that

> drums, dance etc., shut out mundane matters and help the individual concentrate on what is expected of him or her. During Haitian vodou sessions the spirits are called by means of drum rhythms, songs, dances and ritual paraphernalia and given persons may respond to these cues by going into an altered state and acting out the appropriate spirit role.[21]

THE PSYCHEDELIC COMPONENT

The use of psychedelics is a frequent but not essential aspect of shamanism. As Schultes points out, psychedelics 'act on the central nervous system to bring about a dream-like state marked by extreme alteration in the sphere of experience in perception of reality changes even of space and time and in consciousness of self.'[22]

It is of interest that the New World is very much richer in narcotic plants than the Old and that the New World boasts at least forty species of hallucinogenic or phantastic narcotics as opposed to half a dozen species native to the Old World.

Among those drugs which have a shamanic base are the drug Banisteriopsis Caapi known variously in the Western Amazon as *ayahuasca*, *caapi* or *yage*; datura, which is identified with the American southwest and Mexico, as well as among tribes in Colombia, Ecuador and Peru: Mescal Beans, used in the Red Bean Dance of the Plains Indians, the Morning Glory or Ololiuqui used by curanderos in Oaxaca, the Peyote cactus used by Mexicans and North American Indians, and the Psilocybe Mexicana, an important narcotic mushroom used, once again, in Oaxaca.[23]

Michael Harner has pointed out that common themes emerge, for example, in a cross-cultural examination of South American yage experiences.[24] The drug is capable of causing the sensation of aerial flight and dizziness, and visions of exquisite cities, parks, forests, and fantastic animals. It is common for the drug to suggest the flight of the soul in the participant. According to Harner the Jivaro actually refer to the soul flight as a 'trip' while among the Conibo-Shipibo Indians of eastern Peru the Ayahuasca experience allows the shaman to leave his body in the form of a bird, capable of killing a distant person at night. On other occasions these shamans also endeavour to recapture souls lost in sickness, from another shaman. The shaman among the Quijo is able to perceive magical darts thrown by other shamans and which cause illness and death and the Conibo, like the Jivaro, believe that Ayahuasca enables them to enter into the supernatural realms of the world, where they will see demons in the air and other spirit entities.[25]

Reichel-Dolmatoff has described the inter-weaving of the hallucinogenic drug with a shamanic and mythic context. Among the Tukano, the yage plant was created in the mythical beginning of the world and, therefore, has sacred status. The shamanic function is to allow the participants in ritual to:

> return to the uterus, to the *fons et origo* of all things where the individual sees the tribal divinities, the creation of the universe and humanity, the first couple, the creation of the animals and the establishment of the social order. . . .
>
> According to the Tukano after a stage of undefined luminosity of moving forms and colours, the vision begins to clear up and significant details present themselves. The Milky Way appears and the distant reflection of the Sun. The first woman surges forth from the waters of the river, and the first pair of ancestors is formed. The supernatural Master of the Animals of the jungle is perceived, as are the gigantic prototypes of the game animals, the origins of plants – indeed, the origin of life itself. The origins of Evil also manifest themselves, jaguars and serpents, the representatives of illness, and the spirits of the jungle that lie in ambush for the solitary hunter. At the same time their voices are heard, the music of the mythic epoch is perceived and the ancestors are seen, dancing at the dawn of Creation.[26]

Gordon Wasson, who pioneered the anthropological study of mushrooms, has more recently studied Mazatec use of Ololiuqui seeds and Psilocybin mushrooms. He was intrigued to discover that in the merger of Christianity and native beliefs, the Catholic doctrine of transubstantiation had a psychedelic reality.

In an address to the Mycological Society of America in 1960 he said:

> The Aztecs before the Spaniards arrived called (the sacred mushrooms) *Teonanacatl*, God's flesh. I need hardly remind you of the disquieting parallel, the designation of

the Elements in our Eucharist: 'Take, eat, this is my Body' and again 'Grant us therefore, gracious Lord, so to eat the flesh of thy dear son.' But there is one difference. The orthodox Christian must accept by faith the miracle of the conversion of the bread into God's flesh; that is what is meant by the Doctrine of Transubstantiation. By contrast the mushroom of the Aztecs carries its own conviction; every communicant will testify to the miracle that he has experienced

Wasson, who is noted for his identification of Soma in the Indian 'Rig Veda' with the hallucinogenic mushroom *Amanita muscaria*, has published his views that the Eleusian mysteries similarly had a hallucinogenic component. Wasson was impressed by the fact that Plato had drunk the sacred potion in the Temple of Eleusis and had spent the night seeing the 'Great Vision'. Wasson proposed to investigate whether Plato's and other visionary experiences might not have been some form of shamanic exercise. Plato, for example, outlined in 'The Republic' his views on the Ideal world of Archetypes, where the original and true factors of life had their origin. Working in conjunction with Albert Hofmann, who first synthesised LSD, Wasson now believes that the visions at Eleusis were caused by the ergot fungus present in the wheat and barley crop. Demeter's Temple was located close to the extensive wheat and barley field of the Rarian plane, and the Mysteries express a spiritual rebirth cycle linked closely with Demeter's and Persephone's association with wheat and barley.

The initiates assembled in the telestrion and experienced a visionary illumination. But Wasson believes that the archaeological remains suggest this was not a theatrical performance. 'What was witnessed there was no play by actors, but phasmata,[27] ghostly apparitions, in particular the spirit of Persephone herself.'[28]

He notes that the poet Pindar and the tragedian Sophocles testified to the value of what was seen at Eleusis:

There were physical symptoms, moreover, that accompanied the vision; fear and a trembling in the limbs, vertigo, nausea, and a cold sweat. Then came a vision, a sight amidst an aura of brilliant light that suddenly flickered through the darkened chamber. . . . The division between earth and sky melted into a pillar of light.

These are the symptomatic reactions not to a drama or ceremony, but to a mystical vision: and since the sight could be offered to thousands of initiates each year depending upon schedule, it seems obvious that a hallucinogen must have induced it.[29]

Using evidence based on the 'Homeric Hymn to Demeter', Wasson concludes that the sacred potion contained barley, water and a fragrant mint called *blechon*. Since this mint is not psychoactive, Wasson believes that the barley was the source of the psychotropic element, and therefore opts for ergot of barley as the vital ingredient.[30]

The shamanic flight in ancient Greece was not always precipitated by hallucinogens, however, but generally speaking such accounts retain comparable themes. This in itself suggests that hallucinogenic drugs as such are only catalysts for these experiences and do not in themselves produce the cosmological content in the shaman's altered state of consciousness. A detailed account of a non-hallucinogenic trance journey which survives from this period is that of Aristeas of Proconnesus, who is mentioned by various writers including Herodotus, Pliny, Suidas and Maximus of Tyre. Pliny's description is reminiscent of Central and South American shamans particularly and also Carlos Castaneda's vivid account of shaman-transformation into a bird form.[31] Pliny writes: 'the soul of Aristeas was seen flying from his mouth . . . in the form of a raven.' Maximus confirms this in more detail:

There was a man of Proconesus whose body would lie alive, yes, but with only the dimmest flicker of life and in a state very near to death; while his soul would issue from it and wander in the sky like a bird, surveying all beneath, land, sea, rivers, cities, nations of mankind and occurrences and creatures of all sorts. Then returning into and raising up its body, which it treated like an instrument it would relate the various things it had seen and heard in various places.

Aristeas's account of his trance wanderings are contained in his poem 'Arimaspea' which has come down to us in fragments. It details his trance journey beyond Scythia to the land of the Issedonians and then over the snow-clad mountain ranges towards a golden treasure guarded by griffins, sacred to Apollo, the sun god. The poem thus merges geographical components with mythological ones, and according to Maximus, Aristeas in his transcendental state had 'a much clearer view of heaven than from below on earth'. Aristeas is thus a classical Greek shaman who like the Siberian trance specialists was able to gain special knowledge from his visionary journey.

Irrespective of individual cultural factors, then, the common component of shamanic experiences is the altered state of consciousness brought about by techniques causing some degree of psychic dissociation. In this sense it is vital to consider the various methods of trance inducement because they are an integral part of the shaman's journey towards self-transformation.

2 *Shamanic Transformations by Martin Carey*

CHAPTER 2
Shamanic Trance

As the trance condition is induced there is a withdrawal of consciousness from the everyday world and a shift toward the inner world of reverie, thoughts and images. In the case of the shaman it is not just that trance is involved, for this condition is also common in the case of mediums, epileptics and schizophrenics. In the person of the shaman we have one who is able to control the trance dimension and who is able to explore the realms of the cosmos which his altered state of consciousness opens for him. By contrast with the spirit medium who in trance becomes possessed by inhabiting spirits and is often unable when recovering consciousness to recall anything that has transpired, the shaman awakes from the trance with conscious memory of the journey to the gods or ancestral spirits, and full knowledge of magical cures or healing procedures. As the anthropologist Horst Nachtigall has put it:

> An important characteristic of the shaman is his ability to shift his level of consciousness while he is in a trance. His normal consciousness is blocked and scenes from the mythology and religion of his people appear in his subconscious.[1]

Similarly, the Japanese shamans whom Carmen Blacker observed were subject either to a trance which involved violent shaking or a 'deep comatose state of suspended animation. This is the condition into which the ascetic's body must fall if his soul is to leave it in order to travel to other realms of the cosmos.'[2]

Trance can be brought about by a number of techniques which have the effect of transferring consciousness from the outer sensory world to the inner, contemplative one. It can be brought about, for example, by sensory deprivation in which a lack of external stimuli results in an inner compensatory release of imagery; a condition of sleeplessness and fatigue, fasting and suspended-breathing techniques and through hallucinatory drugs.

In themselves altered states of consciousness, including trance, are not confined to specific cultures. Erika Bourguignon undertook a five-year study of ASCs in the anthropological literature and came to the conclusion that 'in traditional societies at least some altered states are generally integrated into the system of sacred beliefs and into dealings with supernatural or superhuman agencies.' She also found that 'altered states of consciousness are universal phenomena which like other such universals are subject to a great deal of cultural patterning, stylization, ritualization and rationalising mythology.'[3] The symbolic components of shamanism therefore vary widely in terms of comparative pantheons of gods and spirits, concepts of good and evil and so on, but the basic methods of trance control and the techniques for bringing trance about are relatively similar since they reflect physiological processes of mind and body.

Siiger has reported a typical case of trance induction among the Kalash Kafirs of Pakistan, a non-Islamic group. The shaman or *dehar* initially invokes the appropriate supernatural beings, kills a ceremonial animal and sprinkles its blood upon the altar and onto the fire. Attention then shifts to the *dehar* himself:

> Facing the altar he stands immovable with his arms hanging slackly down along the sides of his body. Although he seems to be waiting for something in a relaxed posture, his entire attitude is that of tense expectation. His gaze is *riveted* on the altar, and the rigid expression of his eyes reveals that intense watchfulness has laid hold of his soul to the exclusion of everything else. (My emphasis)

As the *dehar* enters the trance state his body becomes rigid. There is a slight shivering or perhaps better vibratory movements noticable in some of the smaller muscles . . . by and by this shivering grows stronger until it is a real trembling that takes hold of his whole body . . . his facial expression changes considerably, he gets a wild look in his eyes, the muscles of his jaw jerk suddenly, often violently, and he begins to foam at the mouth . . . finally he begins to sway, losing consciousness . . . In due course the shaman awakens from his trance like a person who has just awakened from a deep sleep.[4]

Behaviour such as this has led some observers to link shamanism with epilepsy, the shamanic vocation being one which allows the sick person to 'rescue himself from his affliction'. George Devereux, for example, extends this even further in claiming 'there is no reason and no excuse for not considering the shaman as a severe neurotic and even a psychotic.'[5]

The 'epileptic' hypothesis appears to be at odds with a great majority of shamanic situations where the shaman acts on behalf of others as well as himself to enquire about the origins of sickness or injury from spirits he encounters in his trance visions. Indeed the general pattern of reportage indicates that the shaman is not prone merely to self-analysis or cure but usually uses his powers to benefit either his social group collectively, or a particular client. Devereux's views on psychosis have similarly been rejected by other specialists on shamanism on the grounds that the shaman has to learn to control his altered state of consciousness. Eliade notes, 'It is not the fact that he is subject to epileptic attacks that the Eskimo or Indonesian shaman, for example, owes his power and prestige; it is to the fact that he can control his epilepsy.'[6] Nadel similarly says that following his study of Sudanese shamanism he 'recorded no case of a shaman whose professional hysteria deteriorated into serious mental disorders.'[7]

The key factor in the shaman's activity, as we have already noted, is his capacity to retain control of his vision. In contrast to a medium he directs his role to encountering the spirits and gods of his mythological pantheon and learning from them. His trance is essentially a dream of knowledge which leads in turn to enhanced prospects for the hunt, a cure for the sick or the return of a stolen soul. The trance technique in the shamanic context is thus undoubtedly integrative and not self-destructive.

North American shamanic seances, for example, are characterised by the ecstasy of the participants, an experience which has been described as

> Total suggestive absorption in the object of belief, an absorption which reveals itself in a 'peculiar, strictly organised and intensely clear, consciousness and realistic visionary state of dream'. The visions in certain cases have an 'almost dazzling inner clairvoyance or illumination . . . with actual perceptions of light of a purely hallucinatory or physically sensuous nature'.[8]

Among the Iglulik Eskimos a similar phenomenon arises during the shamanic initiation. The master extracts the disciple's 'soul' from his eyes, brain and intestines 'so that the spirits may know what is best in him'. Enlightenment ('angakoq') follows. This consists of 'a mysterious light which the shaman suddenly feels in his body, inside his head, within the brain, an inexplicable searchlight, a luminous fire, which enables him to see in the dark, both literally and metaphorically speaking, for he can now, even with closed eyes, see through darkness, and perceive things which are hidden from others.'[9]

It is also significant that the beginning of an Iglulik soul journey is marked by conditions of sensory deprivation, breath control, meditative silence and then mantric chanting. All of these factors are classic components of the shamanic process:

> then men and women present must loosen all tight fastenings in their clothes, the lacings of their footgear, the waistbands of their breeches, and then sit down and remain still with closed eyes, all lamps being put out or allowed to burn only with so faint a flame that it is practically dark inside the house.
>
> The shaman sits for a while in silence, breathing deeply and then after some time has elapsed, he begins to call

upon his helping spirits, repeating over and over again: 'The way is made for me, the way opens before me'.[10]

Nordland has similarly noted the role that sensory deprivation plays in the trance process and suggests that experiments conducted at McGill University by D. O. Webb on the psychological impact of sensory deprivation states may provide interesting insights into shamanism. In one series of experiments in which students wore EEG apparatus in a condition of sensory deprivation twenty-five out of twenty-nine reported hallucinations. Nordland goes on to say

> It appears to be clear that monotony is the basis of many forms of shamanism: monotonous song, drumming, music dance with rhythmic movements. At other times it can be the restriction of movement, staring into the flames, darkness, even masks with special effects for the eyes. If once a shaman has had such experiences he will forever be convinced of the justification of the religion he believes in and the legitimacy of the power he has.[11]

Clearly in dealing with the shaman we are not assessing whether what he believes to be taking place is true or false. What is more crucial is the nature of his experiential domain: what he perceives, how he relates to it, what he claims to learn from his experience. We have already noted that in trance the shaman, as it were, enters his belief system. What is quite crucial is the extent to which his belief system allows profound insights, transformations of consciousness and identity and a renewed sense of being within the world.

The Eskimo shaman, as we have seen, works himself into a state of ecstasy by using a drum and invoking his helping spirits.[12] His intention is to undertake a journey to the deities who control the fate of the animals. The Iglulik Eskimos believe for example that Sedna, the goddess of the sea, controls all the sea mammals who in turn provide food, fuel, and skins for clothing, as well as all the worst calamities that the Eskimos are likely to experience (storms, sickness and so on).

The Iglulik shaman therefore undergoes his trance with the

specific view in mind of encountering a goddess whose effects have a profound and direct bearing on his people. His dealings with her will hopefully restore order if taboos have been breached.

The shaman encounters obstacles on his visionary journey; three large stones roll around on the ocean floor and he has to pass deftly between them. In due course he comes to the sea goddess's house, built of stone. He must overcome her dog snarling at the door and once inside declare that he is flesh and blood – a reminder that he has ventured from the land of the living. If the goddess declares that the Eskimo women have had secret miscarriages or boiled meat has been eaten – both taboo activities – the shaman must appease her wrath by combing her hair. She in turn releases animals into the sea, indicating that rich hunting and general abundance will ensue.[13]

The trance shaman then returns to his people and he makes sounds almost as if he is returning to earth by a tube. The shaman's colleagues are awaiting him.

> They can hear him coming a long way off; the rush of his passage through the tube kept open for him by the spirits comes nearer and nearer and with a mighty 'Plu-a-he-he' he shoots up into his place behind the curtain: 'plu-Plu' like some creature of the sea, shooting up from the deep to take breath under the pressure of mighty lungs.[14]

His triumphant journey embodies several important themes in shamanism: his trance venture to meet with a deity who represents a principle of causality (in this case whether more animals will be available for the hunt); obstacles and dangers which impede his progress; and the breakthrough in plane which enables the shaman to transcend the space-time dimension of his colleagues.

MAGICAL ALLIES

Having brought his trance condition about through sensory deprivation, fasting, altered breathing patterns or some comparable technique the shaman, as we have seen, begins his journey to the gods – a journey which is visually a fact-finding mission aimed at discovering the cause of sickness, injury, drought, famine and so on. It is essentially a 'dream of knowledge'.

The magical journey is often characterised by the appearance of helper guides and spirits in either a human or animal form. The shaman journey of the Japanese priest Doken Shonin, which is contained in the 'Fuso Ryakki', includes references to helper guides: after several years of ascetic seclusion on Mount Kimpu and thirty-seven days of feasting, as the account goes, Doken Shonin suddenly found his body diffused with a parching inner heat. His breath stopped and his spirit rose out of his body, leaving the cave. In due course a priestly figure appeared who took his hand and carried him up the mountain where, from the peak, Doken was able to see the whole world stretched out before him in golden light. To the north lay a golden mountain and on its summit a throne made of seven jewels. His guide sat down upon the throne and said 'I am Zao Bosatsu, a transformation of the Buddha'. The priest advised Doken that he did not have much longer to live and Doken in turn asked for magic formulae with which to prolong his life.[15]

Although in this instance Doken's helper revealed himself to be of a very high order within the cosmological structure – a form of Buddha – helper spirits do not always have such exalted rank.

Asen Balikci mentions that Iksivalitaq, a Netsilik Eskimo shaman, who died around 1940 and was regarded as a major shaman of his time, was said to have seven helper spirits or *tunraqs*, which assisted him on his soul journeys. These included a sea scorpion, a large killer whale, a black dog with no ears and the ghosts of three dead people.

Eliade distinguishes between familiars and helper guides although both play a similar function once they appear:

A shaman is a man who has immediate, concrete experience with gods and spirits, he sees them face to face, he talks with them, prays to them, implores them – but he does not 'control' more than a limited number of them;

the pantheon of invoked gods, demi-gods and spirits are not at his instant disposition like familiars and usually have a more transcendental function.[16]

The Sym Evenk shamans of the Yenisey Basin have seven spirit helpers who live in the rivers along which the shaman passes. These spirits are fishes, birds or animals able to understand human speech and to speak themselves. The Sym Evenks in particular, it is interesting to note, have replaced the concept of a Cosmic Tree with a system of rivers and rapids upon which the shaman travels.[17] The Vasyugan shaman has a similar number of helper spirits on his journey to the underworld, only in his case a bear is the most notable among his allies. Meanwhile, among the Nanay, the shaman is accompanied by an ermine and a mouse. The following is a description of the magical journey of a shaman to the lower world:

As the trance wanderer walked along the shores of the underground sea he encountered a naked woman known as the Mistress of the Water. She took the shaman as her child and suckled him at her breast. She then took three fish from the sea and announced that fish would be sustenance for the world. The shaman meanwhile continued on his wanderings and at this stage the ermine and mouse appeared as his guides. He was shown a community of spirits responsible for sickness in the world and later came to a lake with a central island. He was told he would have a shaman drum fashioned from branches of the tree.

The shaman flew to the top of the tree together with the young birds on the lakes. The spirit of the tree in human form showed itself out of the roots and said: 'I am the tree that makes all people capable of living'. The spirit gave him a branch with three offshoots for the construction of three drums: one for shamanising over women in childbirth, the second for the sick and the third for the dying. . . .

The shaman returned to the middle world, to people, already as a being of supernatural qualities, capable of hearing and understanding even a conversation of the grass growing on a small knoll. The tree from which the drum was prepared was regarded as the shamanic tree of the middle of the world of the universe.[18]

While the shaman journeys towards 'the axis of the world on an ecstatic journey to the Centre'[19] it is noteworthy that here the shaman is not only acting on behalf of his fellows, by acquiring a means to treat childbirth, sickness and dying patients, but he is also obtaining supernatural powers which assist his own perceptions. He gains 'supernatural' powers; he is to some degree a god among men, and he has a tangible link – in the form of the sacred branch – with the Tree of Life which sustains the entire universe.

DISMEMBERMENT AND REBIRTH

Coupled with the concept of the shaman's newly-found power is an initiatory dismemberment/rebirth theme which occurs in several forms of shamanism.

A typical instance of dismemberment is found among the Avam Samoyed: a neophyte who wished to be a shaman was told that he would receive his 'gift' from the Lords of the Water. The neophyte was sick from smallpox at the time and 'the sickness troubled the water of the sea'. The candidate came out and climbed a mountain. There (as above with the Nanay) he met a naked woman and began to suckle at her breast. She said he was her child and introduced him to her husband, the Lord of the Underworld, who provided him with animal guides to escort him to the subterranean region. There he encountered the inhabitants of the underworld, the evil shamans, and the lords of epidemics, who instructed him in the nature of the diseases plaguing mankind. Having had his heart ritually torn out and thrown into a pot, the candidate now travelled to the land of shamanesses where his throat and voice were strengthened, and then on to an island where the Tree of the Lord of Earth rose into the sky. The Lord gave him certain powers, among them the ability to cure the sick. He then continued, encountering magical stones that could speak, women covered with hair like a reindeer's and a naked blacksmith, working the bellows over a huge fire in the bowels of the earth. Again the novice was ritually slain and boiled over the fire in a cauldron for 'three years'. The blacksmith then forged the candidate's head on one of three anvils ('the one on which the best shamans were forged') and told him how to 'read inside his head', how to see mystically without his normal eyes and how to understand the language of plants.

Having mastered these secrets, and having had his body constituted anew after immolation, the shaman awoke 'resurrected' as a revivified being.[20]

Again, we find evidence in this Avam Samoyed account that the shaman has both a social and an individual role to play in his shamanising function. His trance experiences reveal to him the source of illness and disease which affect everyone but he also gains for himself, via a spiritual rebirth process, impressive supernatural powers. The shaman is intrinsically superior as a result of having been reconstituted by the god at the anvil; the shaman's gift of magical sight and communication are born of heaven and not of earth. Occasionally, in fact, the shaman demonstrates his on-going relationship with the heavenly domain by taking spirit wives from that dimension. The Buryat believe that the offspring born by such unions are semi-divine.[21]

The dismemberment-rebirth theme is not exclusively associated with Siberian shamanism and also occurs, for example, among Australian Aboriginal 'men of high degree'. In western South Australia for example the would-be shaman is put into a water-hole where a mythical snake swallows him and then ejects him in the form of a baby – a sign perhaps that the shaman is still 'new' to the spirit world. The head medicine man now recovers him but treats him as if he were a corpse, by ritually breaking his neck, wrists and joints. Into each mark and cut he inserts *maban*, a life-giving shell which is believed to cause rejuvenation and fill a person with power. In this way the formerly 'dead' Aborigine is reborn to the world of magical knowledge.[22]

Dr Petri who worked with the Aborigines of the Munja Cattle

Station at Walcott Inlet discovered similar initiatory patterns there. Dreams would reveal to a would-be 'doctor man' that the high god Unggud wished him to become a *banman* or shaman. Unggud would 'kill' him near a water hole but his essence would rise up – visible only to medicine men. At the same time the Aborigine would observe a giant snake with arms, hands, and a crown of feathers. Unggud would now lead him to a subterranean cave where he would begin to transform him into a man of knowledge:

> Unggud gives him a new brain, puts in his body white quartz crystals which give secret strength, and reveals to him his future duties. He may remain unconscious for some time, but when he awakes he has a great feeling of inner light. He is certain of being equal to Unggud. Instruction, guidance and experience follow for many months, even years.[23]

The shaman now has special magical powers. With his inner eye he is able to see past and future events and also able to send his *ya-yari* or dream familiar out of his body in search of information.

According to the late Professor A. P. Elkin, a specialist in Aboriginal supernaturalism,

> The psychic element in these talents is clearly all pervasive. It is termed *miriru* and comes from Unggud. Fundamentally it is the capacity bestowed on the medicine man to go into a dream state or trance with its possibilities. Indeed, *miriru* makes him like a Wandjina, having the same abilities as the heroes of 'creation times'.[24]

One could be tempted to regard the death and rebirth theme in shamanism as being specific to particular cultures and characteristic of creation-myth archetypes. However, on occasion western investigators whose frameworks of reality derive from completely non-shamanic viewpoints have found themselves engaged in parallel processes. Although the controversial accounts of Carlos Castaneda's initiatory experiences with the Yaqui sorcerer, don Juan, provide the best known examples of the western-intellectual encounter with mystical shaman powers, there are other examples of similar occurrences in the literature. In 1976 American psychologist Stephen Larsen published details of an inner mythic journey undertaken by a 21–year-old Brooklyn poet named Joel with an aged Dogrib Indian shaman, near Great Slave Lake, in Canada.

Joel discovered that the Indian, whose name was Adamie, used Amanita muscaria mushrooms as a sacrament and was skilled in employing the trance condition for shamanic journeys. In a similar manner to Castaneda, Joel went through a rigorous apprenticeship during which he was beaten and whipped by his master, presumably to strengthen his character and sense of resolve. During his second psychedelic experience with Adamie, Joel encountered animal spirits who tore him apart in the same manner as the native shamans described earlier. In like fashion, the initiation culminated in a renewed sense of strength and illumination:

> In trance I had a vision, I saw a bear. And the bear motioned for me to follow it. This was the spirit, the force I was to follow, to take my journey with. As I was following the bear it turned into a woman. And then there was a whole series of sexual imagery, buttocks, thighs, breasts, a whole swirl of sexuality, of flesh.
>
> I was swirling and whirling, and I felt like I was falling to the centre of the earth. And as I was going down there were creatures on all sides of me. And they would rip and tear, take pieces from me as I went down.

After being subjected to this traumatic destructive process, Joel experienced inner mending, a coming together,

> My feelings were of high ecstasy, shock waves of energy travelling through me. I felt I could see through things, hearts, bones, souls. There was a sound and it was coming up from within me. I was singing a song, the song of my experience, and I felt the song gave me a new strength and power.[25]

Joel's account challenges the view that the shaman can experience rebirth only within the familiar archetypes of his own culture – an issue which will be considered in a later chapter on western trance magic. However, in a general sense, it is clear that the mystical restructuring process leads to new visionary insights, powers and abilities which are normally expressed in terms of the familiar cultural context. The shaman becomes an intermediary between the physical and inner worlds and gains from the gods or spirit-beings privileged and sacred knowledge.

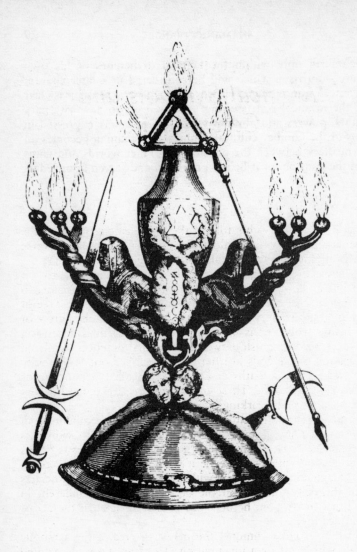

3   *The Symbols of Magic: Sword, Wand, Disc and Cup by Eliphas Lévi*

CHAPTER 3
Magical Symbols and Ceremonial

Modern occultists who follow the Qabalistic system of the Hermetic Order of the Golden Dawn enter a magical universe which in many ways resembles that of the classical shaman.

Whereas the Aboriginal shaman encounters Baiame seated on a throne and upholding the sky, the western magician passes in the fullest sense through the cosmological levels of the Tree of Life and his visionary experiences reflect the symbolic nature of the beings whom he is invoking at each stage. It is necessary, however, to distinguish between ceremonial practices involving invocation of the gods in ritual and controlled out-of-the-body experiences along paths linking the so-called Sephiroth, or spheres, of the Tree. These inner journeys are referred to by occultists as 'path workings'.

In the first technique, the magician feels himself caught up in a cosmic drama and experiences an influx of energy within his consciousness. He becomes the god in ritual by means of his identification with its form, be it Osiris, Ra, Zeus, or Hermes. His imagination is flooded with imagery which he associates with the deity and within the bounds of control inherent in his ritual invocation, he becomes possessed through the act of identification.

In the second technique, the magician creates the symbolic locale within his own imagination. There are no sigils painted on the floor of his temple, no flowing ornamental robes, no ceremonial regalia and no physical magical weapons. These still have an important role but are created instead at an imagined level. The magician endeavours to enter a mythical context created according to the requirements of the Tree of Life or a comparable magical system. He builds up imagery appropriate to the symbolic domain of Malkuth, The World, for example, and then tries through an act of will-power to transfer his consciousness to it, thus producing a dissociational state. His body lapses into deep trance and must not be disturbed. By an act of will the magician pursues his magical journey among the 'god-forms' of the Tree – which also represent his ancestral imagination – and then returns with an account of his visionary experience. Such a journey is then evaluated for its mythological 'purity' by his magical colleagues. The system of 'mythological correspondence' – a virtual 'god-chart' of the unconscious[1] has traditionally provided some measure of reassurance that the trance magician has experienced a valid visionary journey and has travelled in specific areas upon the Tree. Though this magical technique is essentially an out-of-the-body one and produces ecstasy as in the case of the traditional shaman, the factor of mastery is crucial. If the magician, while wandering on the inner planes of the Tree of Life, in a dissociational state of mind, allows himself to be overwhelmed by any single image or symbolic being that should confront him, he risks the danger of being 'possessed' by that image.

Regardless of which magical technique was used historically in the Golden Dawn the scope of magical activity upon the Tree was usually linked to the Sephiroth at the lower end of the Tree of Life since the loftier ones were of a more inaccessible, transcendental nature. Within the system of ceremonial grades the Neophyte was progressively initiated in symbolic experiences pertaining to Malkuth, Yesod, Hod and Netzach and was then ready for the spiritual rebirth ritual which would take him into Tiphareth, the level of consciousness associated with mystical renewal. Similar procedures operate in most magical groups today and the shamanic parallels remain. Like the shaman, the contemporary magician recognises the paramount role of ritual costume which identifies the practitioner with the reality of the mythological framework he is invoking within his consciousness. As will be seen subsequently it is more usual to employ such regalia when involved in ceremonial practices than when undertaking 'path workings', which equate with the shaman's journey of the soul.

Meditative techniques and the ritual chanting of sacred mantra-like god names have essentially the same effect as the sensory deprivation methods of the shaman, namely a channelling of the concentration towards a magical and cosmological goal. The magician within his ceremonial circle enters a sacred space and perceptually encounters the god-images of his invocation. Such chanting of god-names and concentration on the images and symbols of the gods have a profound emphasis on the creative imagination, stimulating the archetypes of the unconscious mind.

As noted above, the contemporary magical approach involves a two-fold distinction. One either summons magical forces through invocation – which then comes to occupy the consciousness of the magician – or else the magician uses an out-of-the-body technique and 'rises on the planes' to encounter them. Both approaches allow comparisons with traditional shamanism.

WESTERN MAGIC IN THE GOLDEN DAWN

The history of the Hermetic Order of the Golden Dawn and its derivatives has been well documented by such historians as Ellic Howe, Francis King and Ithell Colquhoun and there is no need to duplicate that material here. But essentially, the ritual magician, in following ceremonial practices based upon the symbolic stages of the Tree of Life, is regaining the inner, mystical cosmos stage by stage. In working from the lower manifestations of the Qabalistic universe through to the most elevated ones, from Malkuth, The World, to the transpersonal, visionary states high upon the Tree, the magician is essentially employing ritual to integrate the symbolic contents of the psyche.

Like the traditional shaman with his paths of entry into the underworld or hole in the vault of the sky, the occultist endeavours to retrace the steps to the source of his own being. The magician following the traditional Golden Dawn approach has therefore to imagine that he is partaking of the nature of each of the gods in turn and embody into his nature their very 'essence'. His rituals are designed to control all the circumstances which assist him in his journey through the unconscious mind and imagination. They embody all the symbols and colours of the god, the utterance of magical 'names of power', and the burning of incense or perfume appropriate to the deity concerned.

Essentially the magician imagines that he has become the deity whose forms he imitates in ritual. The process of the gods ruling man is thus reversed so that the magician now controls the gods. Like the shaman he is a master of his visions. It is now the magician himself and not the gods of the creation drama who utters the sacred names which sustain the universe. The occultist invokes symbolic experiences in Malkuth which, like the cave of the shaman, signify a descent into the underworld of the unconscious mind and he proceeds eventually through levels which will take him through the lunar experiences of Yesod and eventually towards mystical rebirth in the solar vision of Tiphareth at the centre of the Tree.

Some magicians take the most 'direct route' upon the tree by travelling from Malkuth to Yesod and then Tiphareth via the so-called Middle Pillar. They do not retrace the zig-zag path of the Sephiroth according to the Qabalistic creation process described in the 'Zohar', but concentrate on the harmonised middle way which is neither positive nor negative. Other occultists may choose to follow a more discursive path on the Tree which literally retraces the ten-fold division from Malkuth to Kether. Contemporary magicians believe this route reveals greater knowledge but is also fraught with more dangers, since the occultist leaves himself open to becoming unbalanced psychically on each side of the Tree.

MAGIC AND THE SENSES

Magicians have developed aids for the elevation of consciousness. These aids include symbolic gestures and expressions which, together with certain implements, form the magical ritual. The ritual itself includes 'a deliberate exhilaration of the Will and the exhaltation of the Imagination, the end being the purification of the personality and the attainment of a spiritual state of consciousness.'[2]

Because the consciousness of the magician is to be transformed in its entirety, the ritual must enhance all the senses in fine degree. The way in which this is done can be summarised as follows:

SIGHT   The ritual robes, actions and implements are a visual representation relevant to the specific end which is sought. In this drama carefully chosen colours and symbols play a paramount role.

SOUND   This involves the vibration of god names, chants or mantras (predominantly derived from the Qabalah) whose auditory rhythms have a profound effect on the consciousness.

TASTE   This may take the form of a sacrament which relates symbolically to the nature of the god in the ritual.

SMELL   Incense and perfumes may be used to produce rapport with a specific deity or being from the magical cosmology.

TOUCH   This is developed at a level outside the physical organism since assimilation with god-forms takes place in the trance-state. The magician's 'soul body' performs functions parallel to those undertaken on the physical plane, although the range of perception is of a different order, and may be compared to the tactile universe experienced in an out-of-the-body state.

THE POWER OF THE WORD

In the western mystery tradition, sound and the power of the utterance have been traditionally emphasised as being most important.

According to the 'Zohar' the world was formed by the utterance of the Sacred Name of God, a forty-two letter extension of the Tetragrammaton Yahweh, or more exactly, YHVH (Yod, He, Vau, He). The World or Logos thus permeates the whole mystical act of Creation. The ritual magician takes a similar view. German occultist Franz Bardon writes: 'The divine names are symbolic designations of divine qualities and powers',[3] and Eliphas Lévi notes in his 'The Key of the Mysteries' that 'all Magic is in a word, and that word pronounced Qabalistically is stronger than all the powers of Heaven, Earth and Hell.'[4]

In many ancient traditions the name was regarded as the very essence of being. The Gnostic Ethiopians, in their sacred book 'Lefefa Sedek', argued that God had created Himself and the Universe through the utterance of his own name and therefore 'the Name of God was the Essence of God [and] . . . was not only the source of His power but also the seat of His very Life, and was to all intents and purposes His Soul.'[5] In the apocryphal literature we even find the Virgin Mary beseeching Jesus for his secret names since, as a source of power, they are regarded as a protection for the deceased against all manner of harmful devils. Similarly in the 'Egyptian Book of the Dead' the newcomer to the Hall of Maati says to Osiris: 'I know thee. I know thy name. I know the names of the two-and-forty gods who are with thee.'[6] For it follows that he who knows the secret name, strikes home at the heart of the matter; he is in control, the essence of the god is in his very grasp. According to Wallis Budge, in ancient Egypt, 'the knowledge of the name of a god enabled a man not only to free himself from the power of that god, but to use that name as a means of obtaining what he himself wanted without considering the god's will.'[7]

The Gnostics, who borrowed heavily from Egyptian sources and who have contributed strongly to occult thought, believed that a knowledge of the names of the intermediary deities and devils was essential if the soul were to return to its divine origin in the Great Aeon. An obvious characteristic of such esoteric tracts as the Tibetan, Egyptian and Ethiopian Books of the Dead and the Gnostic 'Pistis Sophia', is that the contents relate profoundly to the after-death state. However, the concepts of the Body of Light, Initiation, and Rebirth refer to a state of out-of-the-body consciousness which occultists generally believe parallels the after death experience. Furthermore it is undoubtedly true that the name, per se, is one of the intrinsic qualities of the encountered deities. An extract from the 'Pistis Sophia', which names the rulers of the Twelve Dungeons of the Outer Darkness, provides us with a clue. Archaroch and Achrocar are rhythmically inverted (Temura-equivalents in the Qabalah)[8] with Charachar and Archeoch as close parallels, and a similar relationship exists between the cosmic entities Luchar and Laroch. Clearly, the rhythmic vibratory patterns of the magical mantras themselves are related to the very nature of these devils on the visionary plane, for the utterance of such symbolic names is sufficient to dispel them.

Returning to the nature of ritual we can say that it invariably involves the invocation of beings or forces through the spoken word. However, it also relates strongly to Will, which distinguishes magic from passive forms of mysticism.

In ritual groups it has been normal for members to take a magical name. One of Aleister Crowley's appellations was 'Perdurabo' (I will endure to the end) and MacGregor Mathers's was the Gaelic 'S. Rhiogail Mo Dhream' (Royal is my tribe). And as Crowley himself said: 'Words should express will; hence the Mystic Name of the Probationer is the expression of his highest Will.'[9] That is to say it epitomises the will of the magician to communicate with the Higher Self or Holy Guardian Angel, a level of mystical awareness associated with the transcendent levels of the Tree of Life. Dion Fortune, whose influence continues in post-Golden Dawn occultism, found the projection of her 'Body of Light' much easier when she was given her magical name. She writes:

> In my own experience of the operation, the utterance to myself of my Magical name led to the picturing of myself in an idealised form, not differing in type, but upon an altogether grander scale, superhuman in fact, but recognisable as myself, as a statue more than life-size may yet be a good likeness. Once perceived, I could re-picture this

idealised version of my body and personality at will, but
I could not identify myself with it *unless I uttered my
Magical name*. Upon my affirming it as my own, identific-
ation was immediate.[10]

Thus the higher vision of the Self supercedes the more limited
scope of the ego and the process of spiritual transformation
begins. 'Ultimately,' writes Crowley, 'the Magical Will so
identifies itself with the [individual's] whole being that it
becomes unconscious.'[11] That is to say the Union is no longer
an aim, but a reality.

THE SYMBOLS OF MAGIC

We turn now to the actual symbols of ritual magic whereby
self-transformation is achieved. The first of these is the place of
the Working itself, the Temple.

The Temple contains all magical actions; it therefore
represents the entire Universe and, by inference, the magician
himself, because of the relationship of macrocosm to microcosm.
Upon the floor of the Temple are certain inscriptions; the most
important of which is the circle. The Circle incorporates many
symbolic meanings but most importantly it represents the
Infinite Godhead, the Alpha and Omega, the Divine Self-Knowl-
edge which the magician aspires to. As a symbol of what he
may become the Circle symbolises the process of invocation, a
reaching towards a higher spiritual reality. By standing in the
centre of the Circle, the magician is able to identify with the
source of Creation, and consequently his Will ensures that the
'ego-devils' or his lesser self remain outside the 'sphere' of higher
consciousness. The magician now takes on a role of authority
in the sense that he intends to subject the invoked deity to his
Will. The god-names, which have already been mentioned, are
of vital importance in this respect.[12] Inscribed around the
periphery of the Circle, these holy names stipulate the exact
nature of the symbolic working. In addition, the Circle may be
circumscribed by an equal-sided geometrical figure whose

number of sides correspond with the Sephirah on the Tree appropriate to the God, for example, a hexagram in the case of Tiphareth (Osiris). The circle also contains a Tau which, as an assertive, masculine symbol balances the receptive, feminine role of the Circle itself, the two together providing an appropriate balance of opposites. The Tau is made up of ten squares, one for each Sephirah, and is usually vermilion in colour, as are the inscribed God names; the Circle area is complementary green. Nine equidistant pentagrams, each containing a small glowing lamp, surround the Circle, the tenth and most important lamp hanging above the centre.

The Circle must, of course, be large enough for the ritual magician to move around. He must not leave it during invocation, otherwise its powers as a focus of the Will are destroyed.

In terms of construction, where the Circle is not a permanent fixture of the Temple floor, it may be chalked in colour, or sewn or printed on cloth. Whenever the Circle is already in existence its sacred nature must be reaffirmed in the mind of the magician, for otherwise the Circle remains a purely profane 'external' symbol. The magician thus traces over its inscribed form with his ritual sword or outstretched hand at the same time considering carefully the symbolic meaning of his action. In the final instance, if conditions for a Temple working do not exist, the Circle may be inscribed upon the ground (in the case of outdoor workings) or held within the imagination, as in the case of the Banishing Ritual of the lesser Pentagram. The effectiveness of this latter type of Circle naturally depends upon the magician's powers of visualisation.

The Triangle has an essentially opposite role. Unlike the Circle, which connotes the Infinite, the Triangle stands for finite manifestation, a focus for that which already exists. Symbolic of the triadic nature of creation and the union of astral, mental and physical levels, the Triangle represents evocation. Like the Circle, it must be carefully constructed or mentally reinforced to impress the mind of the magician. In like fashion, the Triangle must restrain the evoked entity, for otherwise the magician may lose control of the manifestation and may even find himself mentally conquered by it, that is to say, obsessed. The talisman placed in the centre of the Triangle incorporates the seal, or sign of the spirit and provides the focus of the ritual.

Returning to the nature of invocation, certain magical implements are employed by the magician within the Magic Circle. Most of these objects are placed upon the central Altar, which symbolises the foundation of the ritual, the Magical Will itself.

Consisting of a double cube of wood – usually acacia or oak – the Altar has ten exposed faces, corresponding with the ten Sephiroth upon the Tree of Life. The lowest face is Malkuth, The World, which represents things as they are in the manifested universe. The upper face is Kether, the Crown, the First-Manifest, and Crowley recommends that it be plated with gold, the metal of perfection. Upon the sides of the Altar, he adds, should be written 'the sigils of the holy Elemental Kings'.[13]

Placed upon the Altar are certain symbolic implements designed to channel the imagination into a state of transcendence. These may be summarised as follows:

THE HOLY OIL This golden fluid is ideally contained in a vessel of rock-crystal, and in using it, the magician anoints the Four Points of the Microcosm (Kether, Chesed, Geburah and Malkuth) upon his forehead, left and right shoulders and solar plexus respectively, at the same time reminding himself of the sacred nature of the task ahead. The holy ointment itself consists of the oils of the olive, myrrh, cinnamon and galangual, these representing in turn Chokmah (the Logos, Wisdom); Binah (Understanding); Tiphareth (Harmony, Spiritual Awakening) Kether-Malkuth (the Greater and Lesser Countenance, the Union of Being and Created).

THE WAND This, like the altar, symbolises the pursuit of Higher Wisdom (Chokmah) achieved through the Will. Its tip is Kether, the ambivalent first Sephirah of the Tree of Life which contains the Union of opposites, the transcendence of duality in all its forms. In the Golden Dawn a Lotus Wand was used which was multi-coloured, with its upper end white and its lower, black. In between were twelve bands of colour corresponding to the astrological divisions:

White	
Red	Aries
Red-orange	Taurus
Orange	Gemini
Amber	Cancer
Lemon-yellow	Leo
Yellow-green	Virgo
Emerald	Libra
Green-blue	Scorpio
Blue	Sagittarius
Indigo	Capricorn
Violet	Aquarius
Purple	Pisces
Black	

The lotus flower, with three whorls of petals, was placed upon the tip of the wand, the white end being used for invocation, the black end for banishing.

Franz Bardon suggested a similar procedure except that he substituted, instead, bands of metal whose Qabalistic attributes aligned with the seven planets:

(White)	Silver	Moon	Yesod
	Brass	Mercury	Hod
	Copper	Venus	Netzach
	Gold	Sun	Tiphareth
	Iron/steel	Mars	Geburah
	Tin	Jupiter	Chesed
(Black)	Lead	Saturn	Binah

In Bardon's system the Wand is made of wood (especially ash, oak or acacia) or magnetised electro-steel (nickel-plated for protection). In the latter case, the North and South poles are identified and marked positive and negative. The magician may have different wands for varying magical purposes, and like all his other magical implements, they are insulated in silk cloth when not in use.

The Wand represents the first letter, Yod, of the Tetra-grammator YHVH, and also the element Air. The ritual objects immediately following, the Cup, Sword and Pentacle complete this Sacred Name of God and represent the elements Water, Fire and Earth respectively.

THE CUP As a feminine, receptive symbol, the Cup aligns with Binah, the Mother of Understanding. The magician believes he must fill his cup of consciousness with an understanding and knowledge of his Higher Self. As a symbol of containment rather than of Becoming, the Cup is not of practical importance in invocation, but is used in rituals of manifestation.

THE SWORD Indicative of the magician's vital victory, or mastery over the invoked or evoked powers, the Sword (human force) parallels the Wand (divine power). Suggestive of control and therefore order, it implies Reason, the offspring of Wisdom and Understanding. It is therefore attributed to Tiphareth, the sphere of Harmony. The symmetry of the Sword is correspondingly appropriate. According to Aleister Crowley, the guard should consist of two moons waxing and waning, affixed back to back (Yesod); the blade should be made of steel (corresponding to Mars) and the hilt should be constructed of copper (symbolic of Venus) indicating that ultimately the Sword is subject to the all-encompassing principle of Love. When the Sword is placed representationally upon the Tree of Life, the pommel rests in Daath, gateway to the sacred Trinity; the points of the guard lie in Chesed and Geburah; and the tip in Malkuth. Crowley makes the observation that 'the Magician cannot wield the Sword unless the Crown is on his head.' That is to say, force and aspiration without inspiration are of no avail.

THE PENTACLE (DISC) In the same way that the Sword corresponds to the Wand, the Pentacle parallels the Cup. Symbolic of Malkuth, the Heavenly Daughter and goddess of the manifest universe, the Pentacle or Disc, is said traditionally to 'induce awe' in the magician. Malkuth symbolises the first step of the mystical journey back to the Source of Being. The Pentacle is thus the Body of the Magician, which he would wish to be filled with the Holy Ghost, and it also stands for his Karma, or actual nature prior to spiritual transformation.

The magician himself wears upon his head The Crown, or headband, representative of Kether. Golden in colour, it is a symbol of aspiration to the Divine.

Over his body falls The Robe whose function is to protect the magician from adverse 'astral' influences. For this reason the robed (and hooded) figure is recommended by occultists as the mental form of the Body of Light during projection. Normally black in colour the Robe symbolises anonymity and silence and is the dark vessel into which Light is poured. Attached or sewn to it across the chest is The Lamen, the 'breastplate', which protects the heart (Tiphareth). In the same way that Tiphareth is the focal point of all the Sephiroth, the Lamen has inscribed upon it symbols which relate to all aspects of the magical purpose. An active form of the passive Pentacle, the Lamen indicates strength. So too does the Magical Book which the magician holds in his hands. This contains the entire magical details of ritual aims and practice; it is in a sense, a history of the unfolding of the effects of his Magical Will. As such it constitutes a steadfast symbol of power and determination.

In addition, the magician sometimes employs the use of a Bell worn on a chain around the neck. 'This Bell summons and alarms and it is also the Bell which sounds at the elevation of the Host.' Representative of alertness, it thus alludes to the sublime 'musical note' of the Higher Spheres, which sounds in the heart of the perfected man. In this respect the symbolism of the Bell parallels that of the Sacred Lamp which as 'the light of the pure soul' resides above the ritual implements and represents the descent of Spirit into Form, Light into Darkness, God into Man. It stands for all that is eternal and unchanging, the first swirlings of the Primal Energy ('Let there be Light'). It is 'the Lost Word, the dying music whose sevenfold echo is IAO and AUM. Without this Light,' says Crowley, 'the magician could not work at all; yet few indeed are the magicians that have known of it, and far fewer they that have beheld its brilliance.'[14]

CEREMONIAL

As we noted, the ritual magician stimulates his imagination by surrounding himself with a number of sacred, symbolic objects, and by employing mythological principles as the basis of ceremonial. Facing towards the East, he engages upon his encounter with the gods. In the Eastern quarter stands the Censer containing red-hot coals and fuming incense, and which symbolises the manner in which the imperfect lower ego is to be sacrificed to the 'true' Higher Self.

The Neophyte ritual stresses the beginning of the magical journey in an appropriate manner. When the Hierophant, or spiritual master of the ceremony addresses the gathering he says:

> My station is on the Throne of the East in the place where the Sun rises and I am the Master of the Hall, governing it according to the Laws of the Order, as He whose Image I am, is the Master of all who work for the Hidden Knowledge. My robe is red because of Uncreated Fire and Created Fire and I hold the Banner of the Morning Light which is the Banner of the East. I am called Power and Mercy and Light and Abundance, and I am the Expounder of the Mysteries.'

In delineating the magical quest as a transition from darkness to light, the Hierophant adds on behalf of the Neophyte whom he is guiding,

> 'I come in the Power of Light
> I come in the Light of Wisdom
> I come in the Mercy of the Light
> The Light hath Healing in its Wings.'

Although there are several intermediary stages the immediate goal of the ritual magician is symbolic renewal.

After passing through several grades over a lengthy period and preparing for this experience, the magician eventually undergoes a symbolic burial and emergence in the Tomb of the Adepti identifying with Christian Rosenkreutz, the Rose and Cross of the Immortal Christ, and the risen Osiris. The tomb has seven sides representing the seven lower Sephiroth emanating beneath the Trinity which are also the seven 'Days' of Creation. The chamber is situated symbolically in the centre of the Earth just as Tiphareth resides in the centre of the Tree of Life. Spiritual rebirth occurs after 'one hundred and twenty years' which are the ten Sephiroth multiplied by the twelve signs of the Zodiac, and it follows ritually the form of the myth of Osiris whereby the body of the slain King of Egypt is magically revitalised.

The magician lies clothed with the symbols of the embalmed Osiris: the symbol of the Rosy Cross also rests upon his breast.

> 'Eternal One ... let the influence of Thy Divine Ones descend upon his head, and teach him the value of self-sacrifice so that he shrink not in the hour of trial, but that thus his name may be written on high and that his Genius may stand in the presence of the Holy Ones, in that hour when the Son of Man is invoked before the Lord of Spirits and His Name in the presence of the Ancient of Days. It is written: "If any man will come after Me, let him take up his cross, and deny himself, and follow Me".'

The magician extends his arms so that his body forms a cross, the ritual expression of rebirth. He experiences the ritual process as it is intoned over him:

> 'Buried with that Light in a mystical death, rising again in a mystical resurrection. ... Quit then this Tomb, O Aspirant, [whose arms have been earlier] crossed upon thy breast, bearing in thy right hand the Crook of Mercy, and in thy left the Scourge of Severity, the emblems of those Eternal Forces betwixt which the equilibrium of the universe dependeth; those forces *whose reconciliation is the Key of Life*, whose separation is evil and death.'

The magician, filled with light, now comes forth symbolically identifying with Christ and Osiris. The following passage combines Egyptian mythology with 'The Book of Revelations':

> 'And being turned, I saw Seven Golden Lightbearers, and

in the midst of the Lightbearers, One like unto the Ben Adam, clothed with a garment down to the feet, and girt with a Golden Girdle. His head and his hair were white as snow and His eyes as flaming fire; His feet like unto fine brass, as if they burned in a furnace. And His voice as the sound of many waters. And He had in His right hand Seven Stars, and out of His mouth went the Sword of Flame, and his countenance was as the Sun in His Strength.

'I am the First and I am the Last. I am He that liveth and was dead, and behold! I am alive for evermore, and hold the Keys of Death and of Hell. . . . I am the purified. I have passed through the Gates of Darkness into Light. . . .

'I am the Sun in his rising. I have passed through the hour of cloud and of night.

'I am Amoun, the Concealed One, the Opener of the Day. I am Osiris Onnophris, the Justified One.

'I am the Lord of Life triumphant over Death.'

Quite aside from the trance aspect of modern magic which will be discussed in the next chapter, clear parallels between the shaman's universe and that of the contemporary magician are apparent in these magical ceremonies.

The occultist not only operates within the context of an ordered hierarchical universe, but his central reference point is the Tree of Life or Axis of the World which unites the world of godhead with the world of man. Encompassing the ten levels of the Tree are a vast pantheon of beings which according to the occult world-view constitute the mythological heritage of western man. In the same manner that the shaman encounters his gods and derives not only a sense of the sacred but also ultimate meaning from that encounter, the magician similarly believes that he is entering a domain of hidden and special knowledge.

The Golden Dawn system of ritual magic introduces the Neophyte to a process which will bring him towards the light and kindle the inner vision, or 'fire', that Eliade believes is central to the shamanic process. It stresses the viewpoint that causality stems from a mysterious and transcendental region of the Universe and that meaning or reality is discovered by contacting that source. Only through a cosmology based on the principle of emanations or hierarchy is any form of modern-day shamanism possible, for such a system provides a structure of paths, 'spheres' or in the ancient Judaic sense, thrones and chambers, through which the shaman may pass.[15]

We find in the ritual of the Neophyte, and also in the other ceremonial grades not summarised here, a blend of esoteric knowledge and 'emergence' symbolism so that by the time the candidate approaches the grade of Tiphareth at the centre of the Tree, he is prepared for mystical renewal. He undergoes symbolic burial in a chamber linked ritually with the Creation; he identifies with the resurrected Osiris and demonstrates in coming forth from his tomb that he has conquered death. All of these functions have shaman equivalents. The magician in this ritual also clearly identifies with the mythological, resurrected Christ – often linked with Osiris in occult literature – not in a blasphemous manner but in a way which places strong emphasis on the cosmic role of Christ as a light-bringer.

SCHOLÆ MAGICÆ TYPVS.

Mons Magorum Invisibilis

Phantasia

Lumen Naturæ

Thesaurus Incantatus

Non nisi Parvulis

Ro Vaughan sculp:

4 *Illustration from the alchemical and mystical works of Thomas Vaughan, also known as Eugenius Philalethes. Note the presence of the Sun and Moon, the central 'inner light' and the coiled Cosmic Dragon. The magical mountain rises in the distance*

CHAPTER 4
Techniques of Magical Trance

When occultists describe the inner journey of the psyche they commonly refer to such terms as 'astral projection', 'pathworkings' and 'the Body of Light'.

Essentially the trance meditation technique involves a transfer of consciousness to the visionary world of symbols through an act of willed imagination.

Trance in a contemporary occult context is brought about initially by a technique combining bodily relaxation with mental acuity, in which the magician focuses increasingly on his inner psychic processes. He may conjure specific images to mind, endeavour to activate energy centres in his spiritual body which are equivalent to the 'chakras' of yoga, but at the same time he relaxes his body and restricts his outer vision. Usually meditation takes place in the dark: most occultists believe it is easier to 'project' the astral body in the dark than in the light. In this sense the magician, like the traditional shaman, applies a technique of sensory deprivation by shifting attention away from outer visual stimuli to an inner perspective. He then attempts to develop and reinforce the sense of the 'alternative reality' provided by the mythological images or visionary landscapes which arise in his mind as a result of his willed concentration. The following summary is taken from the magical record of Frater Sub Spe (J. W. Brodie-Innes), a leading member of the Golden Dawn:

> Gradually the attention is withdrawn from all surrounding sights and sounds, a grey mist seems to swathe everything, on which, as though thrown from a magic lantern on

steam, the form of the symbol is projected. The Consciousness then seems to pass through the symbol to realms
beyond . . . the sensation is as if one looked at a series of
moving pictures. . . . When this sensitiveness of brain and
power of perception is once established there seems to
grow out of it a power of actually going to the scenes so
visionary and seeing them as solid, indeed of actually doing
things *and producing effects there*.[1]

The shaman's journey of the soul translates in occult terms as
an astral projection upon the 'inner planes' and these in turn
frequently relate to the levels of consciousness delineated upon
the Tree of Life. Like the shaman, the occultist uses his
cosmology to define his trance wanderings and the gods upon
the Tree similarly represent higher causality and a return to the
source of primal being and creation. Because the occultist
believes, following the Hermetic axiom 'as above so below', that
his inner body is a microcosm reflecting the macrocosm of the
creation, his inner journey is potentially revelatory and may lead
to the experience of spiritual rebirth.

The exercise described below involves a magical world-view
in which man is regarded as both the microcosm and the macrocosm. The trance-inducing technique known as the 'Middle
Pillar' transposes the Qabalistic Tree onto the body of man. The
magician equates the Axis of the World, as it were, with his
own central nervous system, which he tries to activate by a
western equivalent of yogic Kundalini arousal.

The Middle Pillar exercise may be summarised as follows:
The magician imagines radiant white light descending from
above his head. This light equates with the first light of
creation which manifests itself in the first Sephirah Kether
upon the Qabalistic Tree of Life. The magician vibrates
the sacred Hebrew god name Ehieh (pronounced
EeeHeeYeh) as his magical formula.
    The light is now imagined coursing down the central
nervous system in a similar fashion to the primal energy
flash which descended through the Sephiroth in the
creation process.

It descends to the throat and is imagined to radiate forth in the form of mauve light:

(Sephirah: Daath, god-name Jehovah Elohim 'Ye-h-waa Eloheem'.)

Descending further, it reaches the region of the heart and solar plexus. It now transforms to golden yellow light:

(Sephirah: Tiphareth, god-name Jehovah Aloah Va Daath 'Ye-ho-waaa Aloaaa Vaaa Daaath'.)

From the heart it descends to the region of the genitals and the colour of the imagined light changes from yellow into deep, radiant purple:

(Sephirah: Yesod, god-name Shaddai El Chai 'Sha-Dai-El-Hai'.)

Finally the light reaches the magician's feet and he visualises the colours of autumnal earth: russet, citrine, black and olive:

(Sephirah: Malkuth, god-name Adonai Ha Aretz 'Aadohnaiii Haaa Aaaretz').

The magician now imagines white light streaming down his left side, beneath his feet and up his right side to the top of his head. He then visualises a similar band of light energy travelling from his head along his nose, down the chest, once again beneath his feet, and up past the back of his legs to the head. In his mind he had enclosed his body which may be lying horizontally or seated meditatively in a chair. His breathing is deep and regular. He imagines that the boundaries of light define a translucent container which is in reality his consciousness. It now seems to him that the container is filling up, perhaps with liquid, and that the amount of unoccupied space left in the container represents his extent of consciousness. At first his legs 'fill' and he is aware of his body only above the knees. Then the level rises and he remains 'aware' of only his chest. Soon the only conscious part of his body remaining is his head, for the rest has fallen into trance and is to all intents and purposes 'inert'.

The occultist uses this techique and variants upon it to shift his range of visual alertness from his outer waking domain to an inner contemplative range of images. Within the magical context he endeavours to combine the act of 'consciousness transfer' with the magical act of willing an image to appear. Usually this image is a form in which the magician will travel upon the inner planes. Frequently, it is a stylised form of the occultist himself, usually in a cloak, but as with traditional shamans, it may take animal and other forms appropriate to the plane of magical encounter. While the body of the occultist appears to have sunk into a deep trance, he wills his consciousness, as it were, to occupy an inner plane image or 'god-form'. The magician may simulate, for example, Horus's venture into the Egyptian underworld in search of Osiris, by imagining that he now occupies the body of Horus and to all intents and purposes acts, perceives and looks like him. Magical records indicate that such transfer techniques lead to visual experiences with a strong existential authenticity. They resemble the consciousness states enhanced by the techniques of 'active imagination' pioneered by psychotherapists like Desoille, Caslant and others, and also the hallucinatory experiences of subjects using such psychedelica as LSD, Mescalin and Datura. The occultist believes that his perspective processes have been transferred to an area of the mind which would normally be unconscious, rather like entering a waking dream. Fantasy and mythological components which arise, as in the 'dream of the shaman', are existentially perceived as real and have the same perceptual status as 'normal' waking reality.

Some magical projectionists claim that a silver cord can be seen connecting the physical and 'astral' bodies although according to both Dr Celia Green and Dr Peter Bicknell who have made extensive surveys of out-of-the-body subjects in Britain and Australia respectively, the appearance of a connecting cord is rarely reported.[2]

As in the case of the epileptic shaman, it is not merely the altered state of consciousness which confers magical status. The occultist has to make use of his dissociated mental state to travel along Tarot paths which he wills to appear before him, and which in turn lead him into archetypal and mythological regions. In the out-of-the-body state he thus visualises an entire Tree of Life extending above him and may choose which of the paths he will explore. Invariably he will be guided by his knowledge of associated images which are likely to arise (mythological correspondences) and also the magical formulae and gestures which will dispel them if they present their hostile and aggressive aspect. It is unlikely that the out-of-the-body occultist will ever choose to travel on more than one path at a time although there are exceptions to this. As in the case of ceremonial grade workings the essential aim upon the Qabalistic Tree is to reach Tiphareth, the mythological domain of spiritual renewal and rebirth. Astral flights up the Middle Pillar beyond this level bring the occultist towards the Abyss, the region of the Tree which cosmologically divides the created universe from the Trinity. With the notable exception of Aleister Crowley, few magicians have claimed to cross the Abyss. This would – within the contemporary magical belief system – entail extraordinary spiritual purity and an extremely exalted level of spiritual consciousness. It is much more usual for occultists to explore more limited mythic domains while in a state of trance and magical records of these experiences show that the visual stimulus used to induce dissociation initially has a strong link with the contents of the visionary experience.

GOLDEN DAWN TRANCE TECHNIQUES

Several accounts of such trance wanderings are contained in a series of papers prepared by advanced occultists within the Order of the Golden Dawn. These papers were known as 'Flying Rolls' and have been republished in an anthology of magical documents.[3] Several of these magical journeys involved a combination of the Tattva colour symbols, which constitute one of the few Eastern influences to enter into modern Hermetic magic and represent the five primal elements of Hindu mythology. In their basic form they are:

Tejas, a red equilateral triangle	Fire
Apas, a silver crescent	Water
Vayu, a blue circle	Air

Prithivi, a yellow square   Earth
Akasha, an indigo or violet egg   Spirit

Golden Dawn Flying Roll XI describes a Tattva vision by Mrs
Moina Mathers as she sat meditating in her ceremonial robes,
contemplating a Tattva card combining Tejas and Akasha, a
violet egg within a red triangle (Spirit within Fire). The symbol
seemed to grow before her gaze 'filling the place [so] that she
seemed to pass into it, or into a vast triangle of flame.' She felt
herself to be in a harsh desert of sand. Vibrating the god-name
'Elohim' she perceived a small pyramid in the distance and
drawing closer noticed a small door on each face. She then
vibrated the formula 'Sephariel' and a warrior appeared, leading
behind him a procession of guards. After a series of tests
involving ritual grade signs, the guards knelt before her and she
passed in:

> dazzling light, as in a Temple. An altar in the midst –
> kneeling figures surround it, there is a dais beyond, and
> many figures upon it – they seem to be Elementals of a
> fiery nature. . . . She sees a pentagram, puts a Leo into it
> (i.e. a Fire sign), thanks the figure who conducts her –
> wills to pass through the pyramid, finds herself out amid
> the sand. Wills her return – returns – perceiving her body
> in robes.[4]

In this account and others like it, it is clear that the visionary
landscape derives specifically from the focusing symbol. The
intangible aspect of the vision – Spirit – seems to be incorporated
into the mysterious and sanctified nature of the inner temple,
which in this case, the magician is privileged to enter. The beings
she perceives, however, are fire elementals, which within the
order of occult hierarchy are far beneath the level of the gods.
From a magical viewpoint we can see that this experience, while
interesting, provided no insights of a self-transforming nature.
Tattva visions, often tend to be limiting, or containing, since by
their nature they flow from a specific focusing motif.

On another occasion Mrs Mathers made use of the Tattva
combinations Water and Spirit. Her account shows not only the

link between the magical symbol and the visionary beings which appear, but also indicate the role of the controlled imagination. Like the shaman the occultist is required to be a master of visions:

> A wide expanse of water with many reflections of bright light, and occasionally glimpses of rainbow colours appearing. When divine and other names were pronounced, elementals of the mermaid and merman type [would] appear, but few of the other elemental forms. These water forms were extremely changeable, one moment appearing as solid mermaids and mermen, the next melting into foam.
>
> Raising myself by means of the highest symbol I had been taught, and vibrating the names of Water, I rose until the Water vanished, and instead I beheld a mighty world or globe, with its dimensions and divisions of Gods, Angels, elementals and demons – the whole Universe of Water. . . . I called on HCOMA and there appeared standing before me a mighty Archangel, with four wings, robed in glistening white and crowned. In one hand, the right, he held a species of trident, and in the left a Cup filled to the brim with an essence which he poured down below on either side.[5]

In this example the perception of a hierarchy of beings and symbols actually produces a change in consciousness. Mrs Mathers uses her range of magical names to invoke beyond the level of the focusing elements until the archangel himself appears. Also present in the account is a reference to a magical name HCOMA derived from the so-called Enochian language. Enochian patterns continue to be used by contemporary occultists to precipitate trance journeys, both in their pure form and in conjunction with the Tattvas.

ENOCHIAN TRANCE

The so-called Enochian system derives from the work of Elizabethan occultists John Dee and Edward Kelley, who met in 1581.

Dee had already established his reputation as a classical scholar at Cambridge and was also a noted astrologer; he was invited to calculate the most beneficial date for Queen Elizabeth I's Coronation. Kelley possessed an alchemical manuscript which was of considerable interest to Dee and Kelley also claimed to be able to undertake journeys in the spirit vision. Dee and Kelley made use of wax tablets called almadels engraved with magical symbols, and also a large number of squares measuring 49 x 49 inches, filled with letters of the alphabet. Near by on his table Kelley had a large crystal stone upon which he would focus his concentration until he saw 'angels' appear. They would point to various letters on the squares in turn and these were written down by Dee as Kelley called them out. When these invocations were completely transcribed, Kelley would reverse their order for he believed that the angels communicated them backwards to avoid unleashing the magical power which they contained.

Dee and Kelley considered that the communications formed the basis of a new language – Enochian – and these magical conjurations were subsequently incorporated into magical practice by the Golden Dawn magicians who used them as focusing stimuli to precipitate trance visions.

Each square was ruled by an Enochian god-name and was bound by the four elements in different combinations. The technique of entry was to imagine the square as a three-dimensional truncated pyramid with the god-name super-imposed on top. The magician imagined himself rising through the pyramid on a beam of white light which streamed down through the apex.[6]

The Enochian square ruled by 'Amesheth' has a large elemental ingredient of water and fire. In the following magical vision, which the occultist Soror Fortiter Et Recte (Miss Annie Horniman) regarded as initiatory, a dominant figure appeared with characteristics pertaining to these two elements: an angel with a lunar crescent upon her head and carrying a cup (symbols of water) but with a fire pentagram upon her breast. In her hand were symbols of each element:

> I made the Signs and called on the Names and begged to be allowed to see the Angel. She appeared with a blue

lunar crescent on her head and brown hair which was very long. Her robe was pale blue with a black border, and a pentagram in red on her breast: her wings were blue also, and so was the Cup in her left hand, in her right hand she bore a red torch. Around her was a diamond of red yods.[7] She told me her office was 'Change and purification through suffering such as spiritualises the material nature'. I told her that her pale face and blue eyes had a sad and tender expression as she spoke. . . .

The elementals were like blue maids, bearing flames and their robes were black bordered. Some wore blue winged helmets and cloaks, red breastplates and Swords and black leg-armour. I was told that only through my Knowledge of Amesheth was all this shown unto me.

The magician then perceived the links between visionary causality and her own context on the Earth.

On this World the effect is that of the floods of water mingling with submarine volcanoes and so disturbing the Earth under the Sea. The animal life is that represented by the fish who rest hidden among the rocks in warm climates. I seemed to see them, blue with black or red specks. The plants are water-lilies, a root in the black mud, the leaves resting on the surface of the water, living the Sun. In regard to minerals I saw a great blueish opal with red lights playing in it; it rested in a black marble basin, and from all sides radiated a lovely light.

On man the effect of the Square is restlessness, like waves of the sea, carrying him on with enthusiasm to some completed work. I seemed to see a nervous [highly strung] person with a pale face, dark deep-set eyes, and thin white hands, making a great effort, willing to pass through fire to reach his goal, a solid black pedestal from which I knew that he could begin to rise to the Higher. But hot clouds of steam and great water tried to hinder him from even reaching the fire. The lesson seemed to me that severe criticism, social difficulties, and heredity must all be overcome before we can reach the purifying fire of Initiation and, through that, the solid ground of spiritual knowledge.[8]

These visionary Enochian experiences were not confined to members of the Golden Dawn. Some time after breaking his link with the Order, Aleister Crowley and his disciple Victor Neuberg conducted a series of initiatory experiments which involved Enochian forms of magic. They made use specifically of a series of conjurations written by Dee and Kelley to invoke a series of thirty so-called 'Aethyrs' or 'Aires'.

According to Israel Regardie, Crowley carried with him a large golden topaz set in a wooden cross decorated with ritual symbols.[9] He recited the Enochian conjuration in a place of solitude and then used his topaz as a focusing glass to concentrate his attention. As a result of his meditations, Crowley had visionary experiences which were then transcribed by Neuberg who wrote down his trance utterances in sequence. Although Crowley had invoked two of the Aethyrs in Mexico in 1900 the bulk of his Enochian workings were made in 1909 in the isolation of the Algerian desert at locations such as Aumale, Ain El Hajel, Bou-Saada, Benshrur, Tolga and Biskra.

Crowley's Enochian entries have pronounced shamanic characteristics. The Aethyr called NIA involves magical flight through the aeons in a chariot, a theme familiar in several ecstatic traditions as well as the early Ethiopian/Judaic apocalypse 'The Book of Enoch'. Another Aethyr, LIT, transports Crowley to a magical mountain beyond which is a sacred shrine where the worshippers of God are depicted. The following are excerpts from these records:

[NIA (Aethyr 24)]
An angel comes forward into the stone like a warrior clad in chain-armour. Upon his head are plumes of gray, spread out like the fan of a peacock. About his feet a great army of scorpions and dogs, lions, elephants, and many other wild beasts. He stretches forth his arms to heaven and cries: In the crackling of the lightning, in the rolling of the thunder, in the clashing of the swords and the hurling of the arrows: by thy name exalted!

Streams of fire come out of the heavens, a pale brilliant blue, like plumes. And they gather themselves and settle upon his lips. His lips are redder than roses, and the blue plumes gather themselves into a blue rose, and from beneath the petals of the rose come brightly coloured humming-birds, and dew falls from the rose – honey-coloured dew. I stand in the shower of it.

And a voice proceeds from the rose: Come away! Our chariot is drawn by doves. Of mother-of-pearl and ivory is our chariot, and the reins thereof are the heart-strings of men. Every moment that we fly shall cover an aeon. And every place on which we rest shall be a young universe rejoicing in its strength; the meadows thereof shall be covered with flowers. There shall we rest but a night, and in the morning we shall flee away, comforted.

Now, to myself, I have imagined the chariot of which thee spake, and I look to see who was with me in the chariot. It was an Angel of golden skin, whose eyes were bluer than the sea, whose mouth was redder than the fire, whose breath was ambrosial air. Finer than a spider's web were her robes. And they were of the seven colours.[10]

Crowley's vision of NIA has several symbolic components which are linked through the system of correspondence to the Tree of Life cosmology. The hurling of arrows is linked magically to the Path of Sagittarius (Tau) on the Middle Pillar, a path often identified with the magical act of 'rising on the planes'. The fan of a peacock Crowley understood as a reference to Juno and humming-birds and doves were traditionally sacred to Venus and recorded in the tables of Mythological Correspondence as such. Consequently, although the Aethyr refers to a warrior clad in armour, there are also decidely feminine components in his vision. It is characteristic that the warlike roles of the chariot is transmuted into a chariot drawn by doves; the rose angel proposes to take the magician to a paradise world of flower meadows and is herself identified with the seven colours of the rainbow.

In a later part of his visionary account Crowley describes the ecstatic nature of his trance:

> I see through those eyes, and the universe, like whirling sparks of gold, blown like a tempest. I seem to swell out again. . . . My consciousness fills the whole Aethyr, I hear the cry of NIA ringing again and again from within me. It sounds like infinite music, and behind the sound is the meaning of the Aethyr.[11]

Then his vision twists around and takes a more hostile form. It now resembles the ecstasy-death-re-emergence theme of traditional shamanism and also the Siberian myths of the black-smith at his forge:

> All this time the whirling sparks of gold go on, and they are like blue sky, with a lot of rather thin white clouds in it, outside. And now I see mountains round, far blue mountains, purple mountains. And in the midst is a little green dell of moss which is all sparkling with dew that drips from the rose. And I am lying on that moss with my face upwards, drinking, drinking, drinking, drinking of the dew.
>
> I cannot describe to you the joy and the exhaustion of everything that was, and the energy of everything that is, for it is only a corpse that is lying on the moss. *I am the soul of the Aethyr.*
>
> Now it reverberates like the swords of archangels, clashing upon the armour of the damned; and there seem to be the blacksmiths of heaven beating the steel of the worlds upon the anvils of hell, to make a roof to the Aethyr.[12]

[LIT (Aethyr 5)]
There is a shining pylon, above which is set the sigil of the eye, within the shining triangle. Light streams through the pylon from before the face of Isis-Hathor, for she weareth the lunar crown of cows' horns, with the disk in the centre; at her breast she beareth the child Horus.

And there is a voice: thou knowest not how the Seven was united with the Four; much less then canst thou understand the marriage of the Eight and the Three. Yet there is a word wherein these are made one, and therein is contained the Mystery that thou seekest, concerning the rending asunder of the veil of my Mother.

Now there is an avenue of pylons [not one alone], steep after steep, carved from the solid rock of the mountain; and that rock is a substance harder than diamond, and brighter than light, and heavier than lead. In each pylon is seated a god. There seems an endless series of these pylons. And all the gods of all the nations of the earth are shown, for there are many avenues, all leading to the top of the mountain.

Now I come to the top of the mountain, and the last pylon opens into a circular hall, with other pylons leading out of it, each of which is the last pylon of a great avenue; there seem to be nine such pylons. And in the centre is a shrine, a circular shrine, supported by marble figures of men and women, alternate white and black; they face upwards, and their buttocks are almost worn away by the kisses of those who have come to worship that supreme God, who is the single end to all those diverse religions. But the shrine itself is higher than a man may reach.

But the Angel that was with me lifted me, and I saw that the edge of the altar, as I must call it, was surrounded by holy men. Each has in his right hand a weapon – one a sword, one a spear, one a thunderbolt, and so on but each with his left hand gives the sign of silence. I wish to see what is within their ring. One of them bends forward so that I may whisper the pass-word. The Angel prompts me to whisper: 'There is no god.' So they let me pass, and though there was indeed nothing visible therein, yet there was a very strange atmosphere, which I could not understand.

Suspended in the air there is a silver star, and on the forehead of each of the guardians there is a silver star. It is a pentagram, – because, says the Angel, three and five are eight; three and eight are eleven. [There is another numerical reason that I cannot hear.]

And as I entered their ring, they bade me stand in their circle, and a weapon was given unto me. And the password that I had given seems to have been whispered round from one to the other, for each one nods gravely as if in solemn acquiescence, until the last one whispers the same words in my ears. But they have a different sense. I had taken them to be a denial of the existence of God, but the man who says them to me evidently means nothing of the sort: What he does mean I cannot tell at all. He slightly emphasised the word 'there'.

And now all is suddenly blotted out, and instead appears the Angel of the Aethyr. He is all in black, burnished black scales, just edged with gold. He has vast wings, with terrible claws on the ends, and he has a fierce face, like a dragon's, and dreadful eyes that pierce one through and through.

And he says: O thou that art so dull of understanding, when will thou begin to annihilate thyself in the mysteries of the Aethyrs? For all that thou thinkest is but thy thought; and as there is no god in the ultimate shrine, so there is no I in thine own Cosmos.

They that have said this are of them that understood. And all men have misinterpreted it, even as thou didst misinterpret it. He says some more: I cannot catch it properly, but it seems to be the effect that the true God is equally in all the shrines, and the true I in all the parts of the body and the soul. He speaks with such a terrible roaring that it is impossible to hear the words: one catches a phrase here and there, or a glimpse of the idea. With every word he belches forth smoke, so that the whole Aethyr becomes full of it.[13]

In his vision of LIT Crowley perceives the magical symbol of the eye of the triangle, which is invariably identified as the eye of Horus. The triangle also links the source of light to the first three Sephiroth upon the Tree of Life which form the Triangle of the Supernals. LIT thus begins with a reference to high spiritual authority. It also contains familiar cosmological motifs: pylons which reach up to the heavens and a mountain which is at the centre of the world: 'all the gods of all the nations of the earth are shown, for there are many avenues, all leading to the top of the mountain.'[14]

As in shamanic accounts the vision begins to acquire its revelatory nature at the top of the mountain. Initially the magician is told that there is no God but he later discovers that his own misconceptions have led him to a wrong conclusion. He discovers amidst a mighty roaring sound that God is present 'equally in all the shrines and the true I in all the parts of the body and the soul.' The magician thus finds the source of his connection with the cosmos. Later the supreme being reveals itself as 'the Great Dragon that eateth up the Universe'. In Hermetic magic the dragon with its tail in its mouth is a symbol of totality embracing the whole universe; in this context it also poses as a magical test: 'unless he pass by me, can no man come unto the perfections.'[15]

THE TAROT

While the Tattva and Enochian systems of trance magic bring about highly specific visionary states a more complete transformational process is found in the use of the Major Tarot Arcana in conjunction with the Tree of Life. Like the Tattvas and Enochian squares they form the basis of an entry-stimulus to a visionary trance state, but because the essential mythology of the Tarot is much more developed hierarchically, the cosmological parallels with the shamanic process are more apparent.

Although there are variant combinations the usual system of Tarot paths upon the Tree of Life is as given below. They follow a sequence from the lowest to the highest, in the same manner that a shaman would encounter them:

The World	Malkuth-Yesod
Judgment	Malkuth-Hod

The Moon	Malkuth-Netzach
The Sun	Yesod-Hod
The Star	Yesod-Netzach
The Tower	Hod-Netzach
The Devil	Hod-Tiphareth
Death	Netzach-Tiphareth
Temperance	Yesod-Tiphareth
The Hermit	Tiphareth-Chesed
Justice	Tiphareth-Geburah
The Hanged Man	Hod-Geburah
The Wheels of Fortune	Netzach-Chesed
Strength	Geburah-Chesed
The Chariot	Geburah-Binah
The Lovers	Tiphareth-Binah
The Hierophant	Chesed-Chokmah
The Emperor	Tiphareth-Chokmah
The Empress	Binah-Chokmah
The High Priestess	Tiphareth-Kether
The Magus	Binah-Kether
The Fool	Chokmah-Kether

SYMBOLISM OF THE MAJOR TAROT ARCANA

The World is usually identified by occultists as the main entry into the unconscious. Depicting a naked maiden dancing with a wheat wreath, this card is typically linked with the Greek myth of Persephone's descent into the underworld. Because in the underworld Persephone rules as queen of the night and the dead, she is also seen as a reflection of the lunar sphere Yesod which this card leads to.

Judgment, in the same way that Persephone in Greek mythology represents both death and life (the full cycle of the wheat grain harvest), this card similarly has a rebirth theme. In the Waite pack, for example, figures are seen rising from coffins with their hands in the air. One of the Correspondences upon this path is Hephaestos, the blacksmith of Greek mythology, and this figure also resembles the Siberian deity who forges a new identity for his candidates in trance.

The Moon typically mirrors the symbolism of lunar Yesod and the crescent dominates the card. Two dogs are shown barking at the sky, one of them domesticated and the other untamed. The dog is sacred to the lunar goddess Hecate who is also linked with Persephone in her deathlike aspect. The card is symbolic of spiritual evolutionary principles and a lobster is seen emerging from the sea to reinforce this effect.

In a magical sense water is equated with the flux and change of imagery in the 'lower', less transcendental, trance regions.

The Sun in some degree reflects the light of Tiphareth which is positioned higher on the Tree of Life. Two naked children dance holding hands in the foreground but are separated by a wall from the cosmic mountain in the distance. A radiant sun shines in the sky. In an occult sense, the children are still young upon the inner journey and barriers still exist barring access to the more sacred regions of the Tree.

The Star, like The Moon, is strongly lunar and dominated by the water element. The naked maiden who kneels in the stream is associated with love and intuition and these in turn are identified with Venus who within the system of Correspondences is linked to Netzach. The maiden on the card of The Star demonstrates the flow of energy down the Tree from a sacred and lofty source. She holds two flasks in her hand, one made of gold (the sun) and the other of silver (the moon). Reaching up towards a golden star in the sky she transmits its life energy down to the world below her.

The Tower acts as a consolidation to the preceding experiences. Linking Hod and Netzach upon the Tree it unites the intellect and rational thought identified with Hod with the intuitive, subjective qualities of Netzach. The symbolism of the card itself is instructive. The tower reaches right to Kether – that is to say it embraces the entire universe. A lightning flash strikes its upper turrets causing it to crumble and figures are shown falling to their death. The Tower serves as a reminder that humility is required upon inner-path workings and is also symbolic of the body of man. According to Gareth Knight, the influx of divine energy from the higher realms of the Tree produces a devastating effect upon the magician unless his personality is well balanced and has a solid foundation.[16] Indian yogis similarly stress the need to purify and strengthen the body through physical Hatha Yoga exercises before arousing the inner Kundalini energy.

Two cards follow which in a classical shamanic sense embody the death/rebirth theme.

The Devil: on most versions of this Tarot card a man and a woman are depicted bound in chains at the feet of an hermaphroditic devil. The devil has goat's horns which symbolise bestiality and darkness. He also wears an inverted pentagram upon his brow which demonstrates a direction away from transcendence. Essentially for the trance magician he represents the last vestiges of a purely materialist viewpoint. Darkness is about to transform into the light of Tiphareth and the dominion of the devil is regarded as a predictable and illusory pitfall, comparable to the tests which the shaman has to overcome in reaching the higher gods.

Similarly, Death symbolises transformation. A skeleton figure is shown wielding a scythe amidst a harvest of human heads and broken bodies. Beyond him, however, a river can be seen flowing into the sun. Contemporary occultists view this as a commentary on purity. Death cuts away the limitations of the earthly bound magician and allows him to travel in a refined spiritual form to the realm of the 'inner sun'. In a very real sense the occultist recognises a death and transformation process comparable to the dismemberment/rebirth themes characteristic of Siberian and Aboriginal shamanism. The process is an initiatory one because both The Devil and Death lead into Tiphareth. Mythological correspondence upon the Tree of Life link Tiphareth to reborn gods of light like Osiris, Christ and Helios-Apollo-Dionysus and these deities are in some measure god-men, intermediaries between the Infinite Godhead and man.

Upon the Tree Temperance is the Tarot path which leads into Tiphareth upon the Middle Pillar (central axis) and the sense of shamanic revelation is most apparent with this card. In the same way that the would-be shaman is reconstituted magically the central angel on Temperance (normally identified as Raphael) stands before a cauldron in which all the elements of man are mixed. He symbolises emergent balance and harmony because from his hands he pours water and fire while at his feet rests a lion (earth) and an eagle (air). Temperance is a vital card because it leads to the centre of the Tree of Life and thus is at the very core of the magical process. The Path of Tau, which is the arrow of Sagittarius linking Malkuth and Yesod, precedes it and gives it special impetus and it is one path frequently identified with the ecstatic process of 'rising on the planes', mentioned earlier. Tiphareth is also identified mythologically as the sphere of consciousness appropriate to the spiritual god-man, a central focus of Qabalistic magic.

Beyond Tiphareth two paths lead up the Tree which symbolise the process of self-assessment and see a reduction of emphasis on the ego in place of the growth of a more universal phase of consciousness.

The Hermit holds his lantern aloft as he scales the magical mountain, and this lantern is identified with man's inner light, or in Eliade's sense, his 'inner fire'. He wears a cloak – a symbol of anonymity – to demonstrate that he is not preoccupied with outer effects so much as inner ones. Also, his path is linked to the astrological sign Virgo showing that to some degree a measure of androgyny has been achieved. The concept of the fusion of sexual polarities in the magician appears to resemble a comparable pattern in shamanism recently noted by anthropologist Joan Halifax.[17] Sexual balance, indicative of the conquest of opposites is a marked characteristic of the Tarot images on the higher reaches of the Tree of Life.

Justice reveals the goddess Venus but in her harsh, judgmental aspect. She holds a set of scales and the sword of justice and has been compared by several occultists with Maat, the Egyptian goddess of Truth, who resided in the Osirian Hall of Judgment and weighed the heart of the deceased against a feather. Gareth Knight identifies this card with 'ruthless honesty, considerable powers of discernment, and not a little courage, but prolonged intention and aspiration.'[18]

On the outer pillars of the Tree are two very significant cards,

The Hanged Man and The Wheel of Fortune. The first of these was depicted in medieval Tarot decks as a villain hanging upside down upon a wooden edifice and was taken by some critics to be a parody of Christ, and proof of the heretical nature of the Tarot. From a magical viewpoint, however, it is significant that a radiant light shines from the head of the hanged man and his 'corresponding' element is water. He is upside down because he is a reflection, and acts as a vessel through which magical energies may be transmitted down the Tree from the Great Mother in Binah. In a shamanic sense this card reinforces the notion that links with the supreme god-energies are not only possible but vital, and the card to some extent resembles The Tower in stressing that the magician's body should be a pure vessel for light.

The Wheel of Fortune, which links Netzach and Chesed on the side of the Tree headed by Chokmah is interesting because it reflects the mandala symbolism of Tiphareth. As Eliade has pointed out, shamanism is a flight to the 'Centre', and in yogic systems, mandalas portray totality, wholeness and unity. Paths radiate outwards to all reaches of the Tree from Tiphareth, which as we have indicated symbolises harmony, but The Wheel of Fortune lying diametrically opposite from Tiphareth mirrors this effect also. The wheel generates energy impulses through the universe and is surmounted by Egyptian gods. Paul Foster Case has endeavoured by means of word-play devices to claim an Egyptian origin for the Tarot, although this is certainly open to doubt. Case writes: 'The Wheel of Tarot speaks the Law of Hathor', thus finding significance in the fact that Tarot = Rota (a wheel) which is Ator (Hathor) spelt backwards. Hathor, of course, was a major mother goddess in ancient Egyptian mythology.[19]

While Case's linguisitc analysis is questionable, there is an interesting parallel between the symbolism of the Wheel and the Mandala as symbols of the 'Centre'.

Linking Geburah and Chesed upon the Tree is Strength, a card which plays a consolidating role for the magician. Typically this card depicts a woman opening the jaws of a lion and it is interpreted to show the triumph of intuition over brute strength

(Venus conquering Leo). This sense of balance is later symbolised by androgyne images and serves to remind the magician that his essential aim is union with a neutral 'Source of Being' upon the Middle Pillar, a harmony which therefore belongs exclusively neither to positive nor negative, male nor female.

Strength lies just below the so-called Abyss, the level of reality for the magician which separates him from the supernal Sephiroth, and the unchanging, causal factors in his universe. These lofty regions upon the Tree are thus of crucial importance within the magical cosmology.

Several of the cards upon these paths tend to reflect either dominant male or female images, and in either a 'fruitful' or virginal state. Virginity is interpreted by the magician to symbolise a pure and refined state of consciousness and indicates supreme transcendence. Meanwhile, the androgyne fusion is also present on two cards, The Lovers and The Fool.

An immediate duality surrounding the male archetype can be found in the cards The Chariot and The Hierophant. The first of these leads out of Geburah, a sphere linked to Mars, and characterises action. The god rides in a chariot through the cosmos, in image appropriate to ecstatic flight, and ruthlessly eliminates negative forms in the Universe which he perceives as if they were reflected in a mirror. By contrast The Hierophant is a more static figure, an entrenched symbol of spiritual authority resembling the 'merciful Father' image of Chesed which it adjoins as a path. A very similar role is played by The Emperor (Tiphareth-Chokmah) who sits enthroned upon a mountain. He overviews the manifested universe and is very much the architect of its fate. The Emperor may be compared to Zeus and other patriarchal deities, but he is also one half of an important union – with his wife and consort The Empress. The mountains surrounding the Emperor are barren but the fields in which the robed Empress sits are abundant with crops of the harvest. The Empress in linked to Venus, but also to Greek deities like Demeter and her daughter, Persephone. A lunar disc rests at her feet and the rivers of life flow through her pastures. In magical terms, she is the Great Mother (Binah).

The fruitful union of the Empress and Emperor may be

mythologically contrasted to the Tarot Paths of The High Priestess and The Magus who represent the virginal female and virginal male respectively, and therefore have superior status upon the Tree by virtue of their purity.

The High Priestess is depicted as transcendental and lofty, cold and pristine, somewhat in the manner of the Roman deity, Diana. Like The Magus, her path leads into Kether, the supreme point of light upon the Tree and a domain regarded by occultists as supremely pure. The Magus depicts a figure who is capable of transmitting magical force downwards through the Tree with his magical weapons (the four elements: the sword (fire), the wand (air), the cup (water) and the disc (earth)). As yet however he too has formed no union with his opposite half for this consolidation occurs lower down with the Empress and the Emperor. The figures of the Magus and High Priestess thus symbolise the transcendental male and female polarities above the Abyss.

Finally two cards in this domain indicate that the magician is approaching the supreme neutrality of Kether and must learn to amalgamate both male and female polarities of his inner processes. This tendency is similarly mirrored in yoga where the female and male principles, Ida and Pingala, are thought to revolve around the central core column for Kundalini arousal, Sushumna. In both disciplines ecstatic flight up the 'Middle Pillar' entails a fusion of opposites. The Lovers depicts the twins (Gemini) standing in the Garden of Eden, and symbolises the regaining of innocence (purity). The path links the Mother (Binah) with her Son (Tiphareth) and brings together lunar and solar impulses upon the Tree. Finally, at the very peak, the card The Fool depicts a figure which is said to be androgynous and is clothed to hide its sexual characteristics. The Fool is stepping over the edge of a cliff, and is described magically as one who 'knows nothing'. This, of course, is a symbolic pun, for 'nothing' is the mysterious domain beyond manifestation in Kether and is thus totally beyond comprehension. The supreme reality in modern shamanic magic is thus a state of consciousness which is not anthropomorphised, is neither male nor female, and cannot be contained by the symbolism of an image.

'RISING IN THE PLANES'

As we have seen, the twenty-two Tarot paths upon the Tree of Life provide an important framework for the contemporary trance magician. Like the shaman he had a clearly delineated cosmology and this serves to distinguish order from chaos. While the magician in trance or through meditation is exploring the Tarot paths there are additional factors which arise beyond visualising the reality of the symbolic doorways.

Since occultists stress the will and regard trance as a domain where the willed imagination actually produces perceptual effects, the technique of willing oneself to rise from one level to another is crucial. In Flying Roll XI, Frater Deo Duce Comite Ferro (MacGregor Mathers) notes that this effect can be produced by a willed aspiration to a higher symbolic level upon the Tree:

> Rising in the Planes is a spiritual process after spiritual conceptions and higher aims; by concentration and contemplation of the Divine, you formulate a Tree of Life passing from you to the spiritual realms above and beyond you. Picture to yourself that you stand in Malkuth – then by use of the Divine Names and aspirations you strive upward by the Path of Tau towards Yesod, neglecting the crossing rays which attract you as you pass up. Look upwards to the Divine Light shining down from Kether upon you. From Yesod leads up the Path of Temperance, Samekh, the arrow cleaving upward leads the way to Tiphareth, the Great Central Sun of Sacred Power.[20]

In this statement of practical advice from a leading occultist to his colleagues a clear transcendental direction is perceived, and the ecstasy of union with Tiphareth is brought about by visualising oneself coursing like an arrow to a higher dimension. Mathers delineates the technique of passage from Malkuth through Yesod to Tiphareth, making it clearly into a Middle Pillar ascension upon the cental axis of the Tree of Life. This technique provides one of the clearest parallels between shamanism and modern western magic.

Inherent in the technique are other factors, also. The Names of Power, the god-names appropriate to each Sephirah, constitute a protection device and also reinforce the shamanic purpose. In this sense willed concentration not only provides the means for altering one's state of consciousness to enter trance but it continues to provide direction once the magician finds himself operating on that level. Mathers further notes that the magician can incorporate Hebrew letters of the alphabet (each of which were ascribed to the Tarot Major Arcana) as a means of intensifying and authenticating trance visions:

> There are three special tendencies to error and illusion which assail the Adept in these studies. They are, Memory, Imagination and actual Sight. These elements of doubt are to be avoided, by the Vibration of Divine Names, and by the Letters and Titles of the 'Lords Who Wander' – the Planetary Forces, represented by the Seven double letters of the Hebrew alphabet.
>
> If the Memory entice thee astray, apply for help to Saturn whose Tarot Title is the 'Great One of the Night of Time'.
>
> Formulate the Hebrew letter Tau in Whiteness.
>
> If the Vision change or disappear, your memory has falsified your efforts. If Imagination cheat thee, use the Hebrew letter Kaph for the Forces of Jupiter, named 'Lord of the Forces of Life'. If the Deception be of Lying – intellectual untruth, appeal to the Force of Mercury by the Hebrew letter Beth. If the trouble be of Wavering of Mind, use the Hebrew letter Gimel for the Moon. If the enticement of pleasure be the error, then use the Hebrew letter Daleth as an aid.[21]

A complete trance vision recorded in November 1892 by Soror Sapientia Sapienti Dona Data (Mrs F. Emery) and Soror Fidelis (Miss Elaine Simpson, later the mistress of Aleister Crowley) survives in Flying Roll IV. It is particularly interesting because it indicates the trance magician's direct sense of encounter with the deities upon the Tree of Life. A blend of Christian and Egyptian elements is apparent, the Grail Mother is seen as an aspect of Isis, and a ritual gesture appropriate to (Roman) Venus is also included, indicative of the eclectic blending of cosmologies found in modern magical practice:

The Tarot Trump, The Empress was taken; placed before the persons and contemplated upon, spiritualised, heightened in colouring, purified in design and idealised.

In vibratory manner pronounced Daleth. Then, in spirit, saw a greenish blue distant landscape, suggestive of medieval tapestry. Effort to ascend was then made; rising on the planes; seemed to pass up through clouds and then appeared a pale green landscape and in its midst a Gothic Temple of ghostly outlines marked with light. Approached it and found the temple gained in definiteness and was concrete, and seemed a solid structure. Giving the signs of the Netzach Grade [because of Venus] was able to enter; giving also Portal signs and $5° = 6°$ signs in thought form.[22] Opposite the entrance perceived a Cross with three bars and a dove upon it; and besides this, were steps leading downwards into the dark, by a dark passage. Here was met a beautiful green dragon, who moved aside, meaning no harm, and the spirit vision passed on. Turning a corner and still passing on in the dark emerged from darkness on to a marble terrace brilliantly white, and a garden beyond, with flowers, whose foliage was of delicate green kind and the leaves seemed to have a white velvety surface beneath. Here, there appeared a woman of heroic proportions, clothed in green with a jewelled girdle, a crown of stars on her head, in her hand a sceptre of gold, having at one apex a lustrously white closed lotus flower; in her left hand an orb bearing a cross.

She smiled proudly, and as the human spirit sought her name, replied:

'I am the mighty Mother Isis; most powerful of all the world, I am she who fights not, but is always victorious, I am that Sleeping Beauty who men have sought, for all time; and the paths which lead to my castle are beset with dangers and illusions. Such as fail to find me sleep; – or may ever rush after the Fata Morgana leading astray all who feel that illusory influence – I am lifted up on high, and do draw men unto me, I am the world's desire, but few there be who find me. When my secret is told, it is the secret of the Holy Grail.'

Asking to learn it, [she] replied:

'Come with me, but first clothe in white garments, put on your insignia, and with bared feet follow where I shall lead.'

Arriving at length at a Marble Wall, pressed a secret spring, and entered a small compartment, where the spirit seemed to ascend through a dense vapour, and emerged upon a turret of a building. Perceived some object in the midst of the place, but was forbidden to look at it until permission was accorded. Stretched out the arms and bowed the head to the Sun which was rising a golden orb in the East. Then turning, knelt with the face towards the centre, and being permitted to raise the eyes beheld a cup with a heart and the sun shining upon these; there seemed a clear ruby coloured fluid in the cup. Then Lady Venus said 'This is love, I have plucked out my heart and have given it to the world; that is my strength. Love is the mother of the Man-God, giving the Quintessence of her life to save mankind from destruction, and to show forth the path to life eternal. Love is the mother of the Christ-Spirit, and this Christ is the highest love – Christ is the heart of love, the heart of the Great Mother Isis – the Isis of Nature. He is the expression of her power – she is the Holy Grail, and He is the life blood of spirit, that is found in this cup.'

After this, being told that man's hope lay in following her example, we solemnly gave our hearts to the keeping of the Grail; then, instead of feeling death, as our human imagination led us to expect, we felt an influx of the highest courage and power, for our own hearts were to be henceforth in touch with hers – the strongest force in all the world.

So then we went away, feeling glad that we had learned that 'He who gives away his life, will gain it'. For that love which is power, is given unto him – who hath given away his all for the good of others.'[23]

5 *Now For Reality by Austin Osman Spare*

CHAPTER 5
New Directions: From Atavistic Resurgence to the Inner Light

Since the days of the Golden Dawn several occultists have developed trance and 'active imagination' approaches to magic which in many ways resemble the techniques of traditional shamanism. Since magic stimulates imagery from the deep mythic resource of the unconscious, it is not surprising that the new approaches to trance consciousness have produced encounters with specific archetypes from the western pantheons: The Wise Man (Merlin), The Universal Woman (Aphrodite), Diana, Pan, Abraxas and so on. And like the psychotherapeutic techniques of Caslant, Desoille and others, contemporary 'inner space' magicians have developed ways of combining the will and the imagination in order to bring about a new range of 'alternative' realities.

AUSTIN OSMAN SPARE: ATAVISTIC RESURGENCE

While the Golden Dawn society was fragmenting amid schisms and dissent just prior to World War I a unique system of magic was manifesting in the person of Austin Osman Spare (1888–1956) who at one time was affiliated with Aleister Crowley's group the Argenteum Astrum.[1] Spare, who was both a remarkable graphic artist and also a spontaneous trance occultist given to automatic drawing and sigil alphabets, produced a cosmology which was totally shamanic in its structure and technique. He postulated a primal and universal source of Being which he termed 'Kia' and argued that the human body, 'Zos', was an appropriate vehicle through which to manifest the spiritual and occult energies of the unconscious. Spare regarded this level of the mind to be 'an epitome of all experience and wisdom, past incarnations as men, animals, birds, vegetable life . . . everything that exists, has and ever will exist.'[2]

His technique of arousing these primal images, an approach he named 'atavistic resurgence', involved focusing the will on sigils, or symbols, which he developed to represent instructions to the unconscious. Spare would condense an instruction like, 'This is my wish: to obtain the strength of a tiger' into a single graphic anagram and concentrate his will upon it. The effect was dramatic, 'Almost immediately he sensed an inner response. He then felt a tremendous upsurge of energy sweep through his body. For a moment he felt like a sapling bent by the onslaught of a mighty wind. With a great effort of will, he steadied himself and directed the force to its proper object.'[3]

Spare visited Egypt during World War I and was impressed by the magnetic presence of the classical gods depicted in monumental sculpture. He considered the ancient Egyptians to have been a nation of people who understood very thoroughly the complex mythology of the unconscious:

> They symbolised this knowledge in one great symbol, the Sphinx, which is pictorially man evolving from animal existence. Their numerous Gods, all partly Animal, Bird, Fish . . . prove the completeness of that knowledge. . . . The cosmogony of their Gods is proof of their knowledge of the order of evolution, its complex processes from the one simple organism'.

For Spare, impressions from earlier incarnations and all mythic impulses could be reawakened from the unconscious. The Gods themselves could be regarded as a form of internal impetus: 'All Gods have lived [being ourselves] on earth', he wrote, 'and when dead, their experience of Karma governs our actions in degree.'[4]

Austin Spare learnt his technique of atavistic resurgence, or trance activation, from a witch named Mrs Paterson who claimed a psychic link with the witches of the Salem cult. Spare also began to produce automatic drawings in the trance state through the mediumship of an occult entity known as Black Eagle, who took the form of an American Indian. Spare claimed to see him several times and, in general, lived in a perceptual universe in which the everyday world and the images of trance and hallucination seemed intermingled. On one occasion, for example, while Spare was riding in a double-decker bus he found himself surrounded by imaginary passengers – an assembly of witches bound for the sabbath!

His attraction to the ageing Mrs Paterson was paradoxical but understandable. According to Spare, she was able to transform herself in his vision from being a 'wizened old crone' to appearing quite suddenly as a ravishing siren.[5] And for Spare, the universal woman was the central image in his mythology of the unconscious. In his definitive magical credo, 'The Book of Pleasure', he noted:

> Nor is she to be limited as any particular 'goddess' such as Astarte, Isis, Cybele, Kali, Nuit, for to limit her is to turn away from the path and to idealize a concept, which, as such, is false because incomplete, unreal because temporal.[6]

Like the classic shaman, Spare employed a technique of ecstasy which, in his case, combined active imagination and will with the climax of sexual orgasm. Spare believed that the sigil representing the act of conscious will could be planted like a seed in the unconsciousness during such ecstasy since at this special moment the personal ego and the universal spirit blended together. 'At this moment, which is the moment of generation of the Great Wish,' wrote the magician, 'inspiration flows from the source of sex, from the primordial Goddess who exists at the heart of Matter . . . inspiration is always at a *void* moment.'[7]

Several of Spare's drawings depict the Divine Maiden leading the artist into the labyrinthine magical world. One of his most central works, 'The Ascension of the Ego from Ecstasy to Ecstasy', shows the Goddess welcoming Spare himself, who in this occasion appropriately has wings issuing forth from his head. Spare's 'ego', or identity is shown merging with an earlier animal incarnation and the two forms transcend each other in the form of a primal skull. Spare clearly believed that he could retrace his earlier incarnations to the universal 'One-ness of Creation', which, within his cosmology, he termed 'Kia'. According to Kenneth Grant, Austin Spare had derived his formula of atavistic resurgence from Mrs Paterson:

> She would visualize certain animal forms and – the language of the subconsciousness being pictographic not verbal – each form represented a corresponding power in the hidden world of causes. It was necessary only to 'plant' an appropriate sigil in the proper manner for it to awaken its counterpart in the psyche. Resurging from the depths it then emerged, sometimes masked in that form to do the sorcerer's bidding.'[8]

Undoubtedly one of Spare's major objectives in using the trance state was to tap energies which he believed were the source of genius. According to the artist, 'ecstasy, inspiration, intuition and dream . . . each state taps the latent memories and presents them in the imagery of their respective languages.'[9] Genius itself is 'a directly resurgent atavism' experienced during the ecstasy of the Fire Snake or Kundalini (i.e. sexual arousal).

And yet, for all Spare's transcendental intent of 'stealing the fire from heaven' his retrograde exploration through primal images in the unconscious took him into dark and sometimes unfathomable spaces. On occasion he seemed to be wading through a base level of earthly Karma; and many of his visions were intensely negative. One such encounter plunged him into 'a phosphorescent morass crowded with restless abortions of humanity, and creatures – like struggling mud worms, aimless and blind: an immense swamp of dissatisfaction.'[10] On another inner journey he came upon 'an endless ruin of cities. The streets were a chaos of debris – the air heavy with the stale stench of damp charred wood . . . the sky dead and breathless.'[11]

Spare's finesse as a graphic artist had earned him widespread praise from Augustus John, George Bernard Shaw and John Sargent while he was still young and his best work illustrates his magical grimoire 'The Book of Pleasure' first published in 1913 when the artist was only twenty-five. However Spare's preoccupation with trance sexuality and the origins of witchcraft plunged him repeatedly into a mire of atavistic imagery which increasingly blurred his artistic vision. It may be that he had uncovered so many mythic impulses from his unconscious that he was unable to assimilate them all. In the final analysis Spare was swamped by his cosmology and his work exhibited elements of chaos quite outside his original magical intent.

Nevertheless, Spare had laid the groundwork for a modern visionary approach. Occultists using 'path-workings' and active imagination techniques in more recent years have been noticeably more restrained in their approach. While Spare was inclined to trust his fate to the gods of his unconscious, contemporary magicians have been inclined to adopt the practice of erecting symbolic signposts to guide them in a more orderly manner on the inner journey.

EDWIN STEINBRECHER: THE GUIDE MEDITATION

A cautionary but undoubtedly effective system of contacting the 'inner gods' has been developed in recent years by Edwin Steinbrecher of the DOME Foundation in Santa Fe, an organisation whose initials derive from the latin expression 'Dei Omnes Munda Edunt': All the Gods bring forth the Worlds. Steinbrecher's approach derives from Jung's view, given in 'Mysterium Coniunctionis', that internal mental images can be animated by concentrating attention upon them. The Guide Meditation incorporates both Tarot symbols, which 'correspond to reality-creating images within all of us' and astrology which 'provides a map of the inner and outer worlds' but the essence of the system is inner contact with a 'Guide' similar to the ally called by the shaman. In 1969 Steinbrecher undertook Jungian analysis in Los Angeles which included using active imagination techniques and 'reworking and finishing' incomplete dreams. He had been reading 'The Secret of the Golden Flower' and decided that the 'secret' was to force mental energy back along the same channels through which they had originally manifested. Accordingly he began to use his skills in active imagination to conjure into his consciousness specific images:

> I attempted to do this by inventing a staircase in my imagination that would take me within to those archetypal images I was seeking. And it worked! I reached a 'room' at the bottom of my stairway, thought of the High Priestess, and she was *there*, a living presence in that inner world, different from the picture on the Tarot card, but without a doubt the High Priestess as a reality in me.[12]

Following this initial attempt, Steinbrecher began to summon other archetypes from the Tarot mythology but had a frightening experience with the fifteenth trump, The Devil, who blocked his pathway and was menacing for some time until overcome by a sustained act of will. After this unfortunate encounter Steinbrecher resolved not to venture on the inner journey without an appropriate guide.

The DOME Meditation favours a relaxed bodily position with the back straight and both feet flat on the floor. The hands rest on the thighs, the palms face upwards and the eyes are closed. The meditator imagines himself entering a cave and tries through an act of will to enhance the sense of its being moist or dry, dark or light. Steinbrecher insists that the meditator should retain the sense of being consciously within the body rather than watching an external body image, and in this respect the DOME method resembles identically the shamanic and magical concepts of transferring perceptual consciousness to an inner-plane event. Like the shaman, Steinbrecher has found it valuable to call for an animal ally who will in turn lead the meditator to the appropriate Guide. On various occasions such animals as deer, lions, dogs and cats have appeared and have led the way to the Guide who, in Steinbrecher's experience, has initially always taken a male form.

Steinbrecher warns against false guides but believes they can be distinguished by asking the figure to point 'to where the Sun is, in the sky of the inner world'. A false guide, he notes, 'will generally balk, change the subject, try to divert your attention in some way, hedge or will simply vanish.'[13]

Like Spare, Steinbrecher regards the Guides as entities who lived on earth in a former time but who have now entered a psychic plane and have become 'humanity's lost teachers'. While Spare was inclined to run counter to the evolutionary process in tracking the origin of consciousness backwards through time to its abstract source, the DOME method advocates focusing on and summoning the transcendent inner sun, which is the 'archetype of the self' – 'the inner life-centre'. The basic intent is to 'place spiritual authority back within the individual . . . its true and holy place.'[14]

Specifically, Steinbrecher regards the Guide Meditation as a series of controlled encounters with the archetypal gods and like the shaman, the occultist must retain control of all aspects of this situation. Steinbrecher notes that the Guides do not necessarily volunteer information and must be specifically asked; accordingly, all archetypal beings should be made to answer if their responses are elusive.

Following the Tarot archetypes in sequence, Steinbrecher makes the important observation that the inner god-images are able to bestow magical powers of gifts, very much in the same way that a shaman may treasure a power-object like a quartz crystal, or a sacred song given during initiation: the Major Arcana of the Tarot, in this sense, provides 'at least 22 symbolic gifts or powers in object form scattered throughout your body. A crystal may be in the centre of your forehead, an apple in the heart, a stick of green wood in the right hand, pearls around the neck.' These are gifts to be used in the outer, physical world:

> If the Tarot Empress has given you a copper rod which she explained would do healing, think of a sick plant in your environment and ask your Guide to bring it to where you and the Tarot Empress are in the inner realm. Ask her to show you how to heal the plant with the rod and follow her instructions . . . these tools are for use in our everyday lives, not just on the inner planes.[15]

In the Guide Meditation system, astrology is combined with the Tarot in order to identify dominating and conflicting archetypes within the self, so that the encounter process becomes a form of therapy. For example, Aries equates with the Emperor and Mercury with the Magician, Venus with the Empress, Gemini with the Lovers and Aquarius with the Star. According to Steinbrecher, we are able to analyse the horoscope in order to identify the 'high energy' areas via squares, oppositions and opposing zodiacal fields; 'unions', or harmonising forces, via the conjunctions, sextiles parallels and quincunxes, and basic archetypes via the Sun sign and ruler of the Ascendant. The horoscope is thus a chart and symbolic guide to the individual cosmos of each meditator.

In the final analysis, the Guide Meditation strives for the same kind of inner rebirth harmonising found in both initiatory shamanism and Qabalistic magic. The aim is self-integration, individuation, a broadened perspective. Steinbrecher writes:

> Outer world perceptions become acute, and the world literally becomes *new*. The creative energy wells up from within and a knowledge of a *oneness* with all becomes a fact of being.[16]

THE 'INNER LIGHT' TRADITION

Dion Fortune had belonged to both the Golden Dawn and the Theosophical Society prior to founding the Fraternity of the Inner Light in London in 1922. As one fascinated by symbolic polarities, especially as exemplified in the black and white forms of Isis and also the goddesses of other pantheons, Dion Fortune developed a sensitive attunement to the inner mythology underlying magic. Her two novels 'The Sea Priestess' and 'Moon Magic' contain long extracts from what amounts to a complete Rite of Isis, a richly evocative tract honouring the universal goddess:

> Those who adore the Isis of Nature adore her as Hathor with the horns upon her brow, but those who adore the celestial Isis know her as Levanah, the Moon. She is also the great Deep whence life arose. She is all ancient and forgotten things wherein our roots are cast. Upon earth

she is ever-fecund: in heaven she is ever-virgin. She is the mistress of the tides that flow and ebb and flow, and never cease.

Keen to reverse the male-dominated, solar-oriented tradition of Golden Dawn ritual she incorporated the magical power of the feminine principle into her invocation:

> In the heavens our Lady Isis is the Moon, and the moon-powers are hers. She is also priestess of the silver star that rises from the twilight sea. Hers are the magnetic moon-tides ruling the hearts of men.
>
> In the inner she is all-potent. She is the queen of the kingdoms of sleep. All the visible workings are hers and she rules all things ere they come to birth. Even as through Osiris her mate the earth grows green, so the mind of man conceives through her power.

Having studied psychoanalysis at the University of London, Dion Fortune became a lay psychoanalyst in 1918 and was strongly influenced by the theories of Adler, Freud and Jung. In Jung's thought, particularly, she found correlations between the archetypes of the unconscious and the dominant mythological images summoned by occultists during rituals and inner 'path-workings'.

The Fraternity of the Inner Light developed the experimental work on meditative and magical journeys that had been explored in the Golden Dawn. An important paper titled 'The Old Religion' written by a member of Dion Fortune's group confirms that the Inner Light members believed that path-workings through the imagery of the unconscious mind could arouse impressions ('ancient cult memories') from previous incarnations.[17] The archetype of the Great Mother was regarded by this meditation group as an anthropomorphic representation of the 'World Memory' a concept paralleled by the Theosophical concept of the 'Akashic Record'. The Inner Light magician believed that the Great Mother could reveal, through the medium of external universal memory, different facets of earlier individual lives on Earth. The author of the paper notes:

Most of the members of these groups have, in the past, served at the altars of Pagan Religions and have met, face to face, the Shining Ones of the forests and the mountains, of the lakes and the seas. . . . In the course of these experiments it was discovered that if anyone of the members of a group had in the past a strong contact with a particular cult at a certain period, that individual could communicate these memories to others, and could link them with cult memories that still lie within the Earth memories of Isis as the Lady of Nature.[18]

As with traditional shamanism the means of access to the mythic domain was through a gateway leading to the under-world. In this case the Inner Light borrowed the concept of the Cumaean Gates which were located, according to Roman legend, near Naples and guarded by the Sibyl attending the Temple of Apollo. It was through these gates that Aeneas passed, after deciphering the labyrinth symbol inscribed on them. Like a shaman, Aeneas sought safe passage in the mythic world by obtaining a power-object – the golden bough – which was to be given as a gift to Proserpine. He also encountered evil spirits, supernatural monsters and lost colleagues, numbered among the dead. Then, having been reunited with his father Anchises he perceived the 'great vision', a panorama of past and future Roman history and mysterious secrets of the universe. Again, like the transformed shaman, Aeneas emerged from his mythic journey a renewed man, stronger in his faith and convictions.

The shamanic aspect aside, the Inner Light group highlighted the role of the feminine archetype in much the same way as Austin Spare had done:

it is the woman that holds the keys of the inner planes for a man. If you want to pass the Cumaean Gates you must become as a little child and a woman must lead you. . . .
It was Deiphobe, daughter of Glaucus, priestess of Phoebus, and of the Goddess Three-wayed who, for King Aeneas opened the keyless door and drew the veil that hides life from death and death from life.[19]

The Inner Light developed a series of guided meditations which, for each member, heightened the imagery of the mythic environment and made possible an internal 'transfer of consciousness' to the locale concerned. 'The Old Religion' describes a series of inner journeys, 'The By-Road to the Cave in the Mountain', 'At the Ford of the Moon', 'The High Place of the Moon', and 'The Hosting of the Sidhe'. The culminating experience is a merging with the ethereal Isis in her 'green' aspect as Queen of Nature. The account is given from the viewpoint of a male occultist who is initiated by the feminine archetype:

> As he watched, the green of the beech-leaves and the faint silver colour of the bole seemed to merge in a form that was not the tree, and yet it was like the tree. He was no longer seeing the tree with his eyes – he was feeling it. He was once again in his inner, subtler, moon-body, and with it he saw and felt the moon-body of the tree. Then appeared the tree spirit, the deva, the shining one who lives through the trunk and branches and leaves of the beech tree as a man lives through his torso, limbs and hair. That beech was very friendly and moon-body to moon-body they met, and as his moon-body merged into that of the lady of the beech tree the sensation of the nature of the season, of the caress of the sunlight, of the stimulation of the bright increase of the waxing moon, and of the sleep-time that comes with the decrease of the waning moon were his.
>
> 'You can merge thus into all life,' he was told; and then he saw, as the fairy sees, the flowers, the waterfalls, the rivers, and the brightly coloured holy mountain of Derrybawn, which means the home of the Shining Ones. He merged himself into the roaring life that was at the summit of that great and sacred mountain – and in so doing he took the initiation of the lady of Nature – the Green Isis – in her temple on the heather-clad hill-top that is above the deep ravine.[20]

The traditions of The Fraternity of the Inner Light have been continued by a contemporary magical order, Servants of the

Light (SOL) whose headquarters are located in St Helier on the island of Jersey. Dion Fortune trained the well-known occultist W.E. Butler who, like her, assimilated a vast knowledge of Qabalah, mythology and esoteric symbolism into a practical system of magic. In his later years, Butler passed the leadership of the SOL on to the present Director of the Order, Dolores Ashcroft-Nowicki who has recently issued a collection of path-workings under the title 'Highways of the Mind'.

The Initial exercise, a meditative phantasy journey embracing the four elements, resembles the psychotherapeutic techniques of active imagination. The following is an extract for the element Air:

> Look up at the sky; above you are the clouds and the warm sun. Deep inside you there is a pull upwards. Yield to it, and let the power of the sun draw you up to the clouds. Let yourself be made part of the clouds. There the winds dry you and make you part of the kingdom of the Air. Beside you are a throng of fellow sylphs; together you race across the ocean you have just left towards a range of high mountains capped with snow. Up, up and over them you go, revelling in the snow flurries that blow constantly from their summits. Rush down into the valleys, sweeping through the forests and making the branches sing in thin, high voices. . . . Ride on the backs of birds nestled among the wing feathers, looking down on the earth below.[21]

Dolores Ashcroft-Nowicki differentiates two types of path-workings, the first which proceeds between fixed and known points and which involves familiar symbols ('active' method) and the second which uses a familiar symbol of entry such as a Tarot card or Tattva but which allows unfamiliar images to present themselves ('passive' method). The first is advocated as a safer method for occultists relatively unfamiliar with magical-journey techniques since the second approach allows for unknown and potentially frightening symbols from the unconscious to present themselves. One is reminded of don Juan's advice to the aspiring magical apprentice Carlos Castaneda:

For me the world is weird because it is stupendous, awesome, mysterious, unfathomable; my interest has been to convince you that you must assume responsibility for being here in this marvellous world, in this marvellous desert, in this marvellous time.

In the final analysis, there comes a time when the magician must venture into new realms of the mythic universe and trust his sense of personal integrity and concentrated will. Such experiences are sometimes referred to by occultists as semi-or unstructured-path-workings and within the SOL system are regarded as appropriate only for advanced practitioners. Examples of such workings which derive from the SOL tradition will be discussed subsequently.

In the final path-working of her 'Highways' series, which belong to the 'active' category rather than the 'passive', Dolores Ashcroft-Nowicki builds the imagery of an appealing woodlands scene which heightens the personal sense of well-being and peace with nature. Nestling in a clearing is a small stone chapel where a sacred transformation will occur:

When you feel ready, close your eyes and build in the mind's eye a door in the wall facing you. It is made of heavy dark oak with iron hinges and a massive lock. Study it carefully noting the iron handle. Now, move from your chair and walk towards the door. Put out your hand and turn the key, feeling the effort needed for it is large and ancient and a little rusty. Now take hold of the handle, turn it and open the door.

Before going through, study the scene before you. It is a wood in early springtime, a beaten track obviously much used leads from the door into the heart of the wood. The air is warm and soft as if after a shower, the scent of damp earth and moss all around you. Step through the door and walk a few paces forward then turn and look behind you. The door is half open, the room beyond is dim and hazy. Above the door is carved your name in letters of gold. You are clad in a long cloak of grey wool with a hood that is thrown back and fastened at the throat with circular clasp which, when closed brings together an equal armed cross engraved within it.

Take the path and walk through the wood, try and record the scents and sounds around you. Birds singing very clearly as they do after rain, the feel of wet branches and leaves as they brush against your face and hair. The softness of damp earth beneath your feet. The whole wood is carpeted with wild flowers, see if you can name them. On the branches there are tight green buds just beginning to form.

As you walk another sound comes to the ear, the chime of bells. Follow it and the track leads you to a large clearing in which stands a small chapel of grey stone. The bells fall silent and you wait. To the door of the chapel comes a friar clad in a white robe. The face is neither young nor old, austere yet with untold compassion and understanding in the eyes. He opens the door wide and gestures to you to come into the chapel.

Inside all is light and the full glory of the stained glass is visible. It is sparsely furnished, no pews, just a high backed chair facing the altar with a small wooden bench in front of it. On the Altar all is ready and waiting. Take your place in the chair and make your own prayer. On the Altar there is a silver chalice, small and plain and in a covered dish the Holy Water. The Eastern Window is in shades of Rose and Gold with touches of Blue and Green. The Central theme is a child holding a dove in His hands. The priest comes from behind you carrying what seems to be another chalice, but covered with white silk. This he places with great care on the Altar, the cover is constantly stirring as if in a gentle breeze, the scent of roses fills the chapel and though no-one else is present there is an unheard song of praise that fills the inner ear.

Kneel now at the bench and prepare yourself to become a receiver. Empty yourself as completely as you can, leaving the mind, not blank but 'ready'. The priest comes to you with the communion which you take. He then departs from the chapel taking the small chalice and the plate with him.

Take your seat again and fix your eyes on the covered object on the altar. Now, in this state, *already* on a higher level than the physical, go into a meditation thus passing into the next level. Let the covered chalice be your doorway. It becomes larger until it fills your vision, its shape shining through the cloth. Let 'It' fill your mind, which you have emptied ready for whatever may come. Try and grasp what is being impressed on your highered state of consciousness.

Gradually the Grail returns to its former size and the chapel becomes visible around you once more. Hold on to whatever it is that has been passed to you. Make your thanks and go to the door, pause there and look back. All the light within the chapel is coming from the covered Grail and a low musical humming sound fills the air.

Outside all is quiet and peaceful, just a lovely wood full of flowers. Retrace your steps until you come to the door, go through it closing and locking it behind you. Sit down in the chair. Feel the physical body close around you and when you are ready open your eyes. Record your 'Grail message' at once before you forget. This may take time and tire you a bit for you are passing through the astral to the mental plane using one as a stepping stone to the other, but a short rest should be enough to restore you.[22]

Since the Servants of Light operates a system of magical training through correspondence it has extended its direct international influence further than the Golden Dawn, which had Temples only in Britain and France, and affiliated Orders in the United States. The SOL currently has practising members in the United States, Germany, Nigeria, Ghana, Zambia, Ethiopia, Britain and Australia. Dolores Ashcroft-Nowicki has been able to maintain the core structure of SOL magical procedure by periodically visiting the main centres of occult activity.

In Sydney a group of SOL trained occultists, including 'Magus' editors Catherine Colefax and Cheryl Weeks, and psycho-mythologist Moses Aaron began a series of more complex magical path-workings based on specific cosmic archetypes. All three had worked extensively in communicating with different aspects of the Goddess. Catherine Colefax and Cheryl Weeks had developed Dion Fortune's 'Rite of Isis' to embrace path-workings invoking images of Demeter, Persephone, Diana, Aphrodite and the Black Isis, and Moses Aaron had had extensive inner plane magical contact with a number of magical entities including the venerable Merlin and the Minotaur-guardian of the Labyrinth.

The approach of the 'Magus' phantasy group was collectively to prepare 'entry meditations' which would summon appropriate archetypal images to mind and establish a point of contact with the mythic plane. One member of the group would read the entry aloud, much in the same fashion as Robert Masters's and Jean Houston's 'mind game' technique, while the others would build the inner sensation of the alternative, symbolic reality as a locale for transferring consciousness. In some cases the entry sequences were reasonably brief, in other instances complex and detailed. However, having entered the mythic space, one then had to complete the journey unaided, recalling contact with the archetypes in as much detail as possible so that the magical encounters could be systematically recorded immediately afterwards. These journeys thus belonged to the second order of path-workings, which did not lead between specific symbolic points of entry and departure, but included spontaneous intangibles. The entry for an early phantasy journey, invoking Pan, was reasonably brief:

> Go through the doorway. You are on a rocky landscape – flat and black rock. You come to a wide abyss. As you stand there you hear the sound of a flute. The sounds become golden circles of light that make stepping-stones across the abyss. If you wish, cross the abyss on the golden stepping-stones and go in search of the one who makes the music.

For Moses Aaron, this entry produced a remarkable mythic contact in which he was able to converse on a person to person basis with Pan. An interesting aspect of the encounter is Pan's music – a type of 'soundless sound'; reminiscent of Zen:

I cross and come to Pan (Golden bottom half, top half white with golden hair and beard),

'Lord of the Dance, Piper at the Gates of Dawn, I would see you if it is permitted.'

'Then come and kneel before me' (I kneel), 'Now look up' I see Pan and embrace him.

'Lord I would be comforted by you.' (He picks me up like a child on his left arm) 'Lord I would kiss you' (I kiss him on the mouth feeling incredibly joyful being held by him).

'It is time to go.'

'Lord I would be held a little longer by you. When I am in your arms I am comforted and do not fear.'

'What is your fear?'

'Lord I do not know, but in your arms I am protected from all fear.'

'In that you are wrong little one. I can protect you perhaps from all the outer fear but the true fear that is inside you, not I nor any being can protect you from, except your star – now it is time to go.'

'Lord Piper if it is permitted, play your pipe for me.' (He plays it)

'Little one, what did you hear?'

'I heard nothing Lord.'

'The sweetest music is that which is unheard.'

'Lord that sounds like a vile paradox.'

' – or an inexpressible truth. Which is it for you?'

'Lord I don't know. Play your pipe again.' (Again I hear nothing.)

'Now it is time to go.' (He puts me down. I hold his hand and we walk back to the abyss.)

'Lord can you walk on the golden discs?'

'I can but I have no need.' (He picks me up and holding me in his arms he leaps across the abyss – and puts me down on the other side.)

'Lord I would visit you again if it is permitted.'

'It is certainly permitted. Till then, good listening, little one.'

Some of the original semi-structured magical journeys of the 'Magus' group included encounters with Diana, the Guardian of the Ring Stones (modelled on Stonehenge, but featuring twelve stones for each sign of the Zodiac, each vibrating a musical note) and a mythic quest for buried treasure (the 'inner gold').

During this time I had been involved with more structured path-workings involving the initiatory archetypes of the Tarot. I had prepared a series of 'mind game' voyages embracing the 22 Major Arcana and leading from The World through to the paradoxical card of The Fool, and this had been included in an earlier book 'Don Juan, Mescalito and Modern Magic'. By experimenting with synthesiser music I had arranged a series of meditation tapes which double-tracked the Tarot path-workings over the evocative textural 'inner space' music of such instrumentalists as Klaus Schulze, Edgar Froese, Brian Eno, Manuel Gottsching and others, most of whom belonged to the German electronic-music genre, or had been influenced by it.

Appreciating the potentially far-reaching nature of semi-structured magical path-workings, I joined the 'Magus' phantasy group from their fourth journey onwards. With the Tarot material I had been running the risk, within John Lilly's terminology, of confining my range of perceptions to my own belief system – in other words, imposing unnecessary limitations. The 'Magus' path-workings since that time have been more far reaching and have included more diverse content.

Building on the Goddess-orientation of the three other participants, a magical entry was prepared for an encounter with The Empress, an archetypal Goddess who, of course, is present in the Tarot but is universally represented in mythology as the Mother of the Universe. Optional sequences were included within the path-working to allow each person to individualise the contact with the Goddess:

We enter a cave door and descend by a flight of ancient

stone steps to the palace of the Empress. At the bottom of
the steps we come to a magnificent door encrusted with
silver discs and beautiful sea-blue gemstones. The door
swings in and we enter the ante-chamber. The floor is
pearly and translucent and the walls of the chamber
shimmer shimmer like starlit mirrors.

A young maiden presents herself as mistress of the star-
chamber and we tell her we would like to meet the
Empress. The maiden says that she may allow us to enter
one of three doorways and that she will give us a gift to
enable us to be effective in the goddess's domain. The gifts
are:

> a scythe with which to harvest wheat
> a silver goblet from which to drink
> a luminous crystal to guide us beneath a lake

We see symbols of these on doorways before us and take
our gifts to enter. We are told that as a summation of our
experience we will meet the Empress and should account
for ourselves, telling her in what manner we have travelled
in her domain and what we have learnt. And now we step
forward.

My own journey included certain features which resembled the
Guide Meditation. A travelling companion (a coiled dragon)
appeared who led me past potential adversaries. As with the
Guide Meditation, I was given a gift by the Goddess:

> In the ante-chamber the gift I nominated from the maiden
> was the goblet from which to drink. Almost immediately
> I was aware that I was in a different domain. I was travel-
> ling on a precipitous mountain track which climbed peril-
> ously above me on a very vertical incline. I had a guide –
> a youth with a beautifully proportioned body and superb
> golden hair – who carried a fiery torch. The glow lit the
> landscape and it was craggy, with bluish green colouring
> and potentially very hard to climb. I seemed to follow the
> light rather than watch where my feet were.
> Then I was aware of a coiled dragon above me but

curved round the central axis of the mountain. A warrior
slew the dragon and then his own head was cut off. I
didn't see how this occurred but a sense of self-sacrifice
was implied. I passed by and came towards the great
Empress, seated on her throne. She had long flowing
golden hair but I found it difficult to focus on her face as
if her eyes were in many places at once.

She held out another flask for me to drink from – indeed
I was not aware of actually having taken the goblet from
the maiden in the first place and maybe the sacred drink
was the goal – not a gift given initially. I drank, and as
the fluid poured into me I felt I was expanding and could
almost float away. It was a very liberating, expansive
feeling and it seemed that something precious had been
given to me.

Exploratory path-workings in the group have since included
journeys involving the dualism of the Tao used as a doorway,
a new Minotaur entry and a phantasy journey to the domain
of Abraxas, the Gnostic high god who contained the polar
opposites and was also god of Time. While this work is still
continuing and it is perhaps inappropriate to analyse the
visionary journeys too deeply at this stage our feeling is that the
semi-structured path-working allows spontaneous manifestations of unconscious mythology to arise within a creative and
meaningful context. On occasion the experiences have shown
considerable parallels with the primal myths of the shamans;
Cheryl Weeks's journey resulting from an encounter with the
Cosmic Dragon is reminiscent of the South American shamanic
experiences reported by Michael Harner. The Dragon introduces
the meditator to elemental processes in the universe which
exhibit extraordinary beauty:

[The entry was as follows]:
Relax slowly until your body grows heavier and heavier,
and you lose awareness of it with the exception of the
centre of the forehead. Here a pinpoint of light begins to
form. . . . It gradually expands till it covers you and the
space around you, and it seems as though you float in this

light for an eternity. Then suddenly it focuses into a beam that extends about twenty feet in front of you; you concentrate on its tip and as you do, the beam itself vanishes, and the point you are watching is all that remains. It is dark all around you and it is hard at first to see your surroundings. But you become aware that this point of light is the pupil of a huge golden eye. As you begin to see more clearly you see the shape of an enormous body stretching into the depths of the cavern you now find yourself in. And finally, as your eyes complete their adjustment you see that this enormous shape is a gigantic dragon, who is lying about twenty feet from where you stand.

Its wings, which are half unfurled, are incredibly beautiful – a mosaic of living colours: vermilion, deep rich blues, azure, flaming gold, interlaced with many vibrant hues. His enormous body is scaled with bronze metallic patterns that are woven shapes that seem to writhe and dance as he breathes, and along his spine are crystal spikes that catch the light that explodes from time to time from the back of the cavern.

He stares unwinkingly with his huge eyes and you are trapped in his gaze. Your limbs freeze; he watches but does not show any interest in your paralysis. The silence around you is a tangible sound: you wait, and then slowly he begins to move towards you. And still you cannot move, your gaze is locked to his, for you did not know that to look into a dragon's eyes puts you under his spell. He looks deep within you, further than you yourself have been, and then far beyond. There is something alien and incredibly ancient about his gaze, and you feel your transience compared to his ancient lineage. He stops about ten feet in front of you.

You find you are at last able to move. And if you wish, you can choose to leave. All you have to do is close your eyes and activate the point of light in your forehead, build it outwards to encompass you, float for a while, then open your eyes and you will be back in familiar surroundings. He awaits your decision. It's up to you.

[The journey itself]:

I sang to the dragon – a song of evenings in Spring with the full moon gracefully rising and the gentle wind bending with flower filled grass. And as I sang the images formed so that we were experiencing them.

Then the dragon sang, in a rumbling hum, and he sang of primeval forests and flaming volcanos and the hot breath of the wind over an orange sea. And these too we experienced.

Again the dragon sang, a new song, and a woman began to form. I joined his singing. And he sang her a dress of lustrous silver, and I sang her flowing silver hair, and when we had finished she stood very beautiful, a little like a silver fish in the cling of her shining dress.

Then I felt she must have a mate, so I began to sing again and the dragon joined me. And we sang a man of golden beauty, his hair a halo of shimmering sun.

We watched and they moved together. They became two pillars, shining gold and lustrous silver. And they became molten and intertwined, then blended and vanished, fountaining upward and fading away.

The dragon, as I stood beside him, breathed searing flames and clouds of smoke. They remained, and formed a lotus of fire with smoke wreaths of leaves at its base. The lotus opened to reveal a child, who held out his hand in which was a large shining pearl. Then this vision too fountained upwards and dissolved.

I knelt on the floor and dug into the black earth. I mixed it with water and anointed my whole body. It became like an oil which stained my skin.

I said 'I am black, my lord'. I commenced to spin until I lost consciousness and awoke.

POSTSCRIPT
Why the Shaman?

The essential aim of this book has been to show some of the interesting parallels that occur between traditional shamanism and the more visionary aspects of magic in modern western society. It is probably appropriate for me to explain why I undertook such a comparative study in the first place.

As Michael Harner notes in his exemplary work, 'The Way of the Shaman', we have been content in our contemporary scientific world to pass over the folk-wisdom of shamanic cultures, ostensibly because the societies from which these beliefs flow are unsophisticated and technologically simple. In the same way that western doctors have only recently had to confront the Taoist belief system underlying Chinese acupuncture – since for surgical anaesthesia the technique itself obviously works – so too shamanism has provided an alternative body of knowledge pertaining to altered states of consciousness.

Our society does not normally operate in such an 'altered state': indeed the fabric of technology, management planning and industrial production would collapse if shamans rather than scientists, engineers and operations controllers were running things! However, our technological strength in modern society has been our mythological undoing. Deus is now firmly within the machine, rather than ex machina. Our dominant frameworks of knowledge have been those postulated by philosophers and scientists drawing on the latest advances in chemistry, biology, physics and mathematics. Anything smacking vaguely of 'prescience' has been firmly relegated to the domain of superstition and wrong thinking. Indeed, two pre-eminent figures in the history of twentieth-century thought, Sigmund Freud and Jacob Bronowski, were both most anxious to denounce occult and metaphysical approaches and remove them as thoroughly as possible from any incursion into contemporary systems of knowledge.

The revival of modern western magic and the renewed interest in 'native' cosmologies and shamanism as found among the Amer-indian cultures, for example, show that a 'mythic back-lash' has taken place. It has proven to be unsatisfactory, and indeed possibly pathological, to attempt to repress the vestiges of mythological thought in modern man in the vain hope of eliminating 'superstition' with the advance of science. Clearly we humans require domains of mystery; we need to know where the sacred aspects of life may be found and how to understand the intuitive, infinite and profoundly meaningful visionary moments which arise in all of us at different times.

And yet our dominant western culture is hardly supportive in this regard. We are surrounded by an urban technology which has done its best to demystify the world. Stanley Hopper has written, appropriately, of the 'impoverishment of symbols' from which we have all been suffering and notes that in our consumer culture, mythological traditions have been so inverted that

> Ahura Mazda is known today as an electric light bulb, the spirit Mercury is the name of an automobile and Pegasus, splendid in the antique sky, though recognised almost everywhere today is recognised nevertheless in the diminished guise of the Flying Red Horse — trademark for a gasoline.[1]

By contrast both shamanism and magic offer techniques of approaching the visionary sources of our culture. Both systems of thought structure the universe in ways that are deeply and symbolically meaningful and which fully accommodate enlarged horizons of human consciousness. We learn how to transform the profane world and be reborn in the cosmos.

Why shamanism? Why magic? We need them both.

APPENDIX A
Shamanism, Magic and the Study of Consciousness

Shamanism and modern trance magic are multi-faceted phenomena and consequently it is necessary to draw on a wide range of source areas to throw light on the processes involved. Anthropologists Reinhard and Bourguignon have appropriately introduced the notion of altered states of consciousness into the discussion of shamanism and such states also involve consideration of right and left brain-hemisphere research, electroencephalograph monitorings of brain wave functions (EEGs) and the effect of sensory deprivation on consciousness. Several shamans report dissociational effects comparable to those found in the so-called, out-of-the-body experience (OOBE), and these have been recently studied by a number of psychologists who variously describe them as perceptual extensions of consciousness or schizophrenic aberrations. Several depth psychologists have also made a study of mythological and symbolic states of mind which clearly pertain to the shamanic process. Some of these findings have been adapted into techniques of 'active imagination' in psychotherapy and acquire aspects of the more traditional trance journey. While contemporary magicians are likely to refer to Jungian frameworks of archetypal psychology as their basis for analysis, recent work on 'programmes of belief' in the unconscious mind are also vitally relevant. Such studies emphasise the scope that a given belief system provides for the expansion of consciousness and visionary perspectives.

PHYSIOLOGY AND MYSTICISM

An immediate consideration is whether shamans and trance magicians fall into the broad category of mystics. Mysticism has been defined by J. H. Leuba as 'an experience taken by the experiencer to be an immediate contact or union of the self with the "larger-than-self" be it called the World Spirit, God the Absolute or whatever,'[1] and Evelyn Underhill in her definitive work 'Mysticism' describes the phenomenon as 'establishing one's conscious relation with the Absolute'.[2] We have already indicated that the shaman operates within a defined cosmos and encounters as an existential reality the deities and Spirit beings who for him have supreme meaning in his culture. Frequently, the gods of the shaman are those who uphold life, who hold the keys to prosperity and the antidotes for disease and evil. In this sense it is appropriate to regard the shamanic journey as a quest involving contact with the absolute. Ehrenwald has even described the out-of-the-body experience which is an integral part of shamanism as 'an expression of man's perennial quest for immortality . . . a faltering attempt to assert the reality and autonomous existence of the "soul" – a deliberate challenge to the threat of extinction.'[3] Clearly such processes *are* involved. The shaman as in intermediary between mankind and the gods has access to planes of existence not normally accessible to the living and he frequently demonstrates through the 'death and re-emergence' process that he is capable of transcending mortality.

Harriet Whitehead similarly concludes that the mystic and magician share many features in common and that their activities lie on a continuum:

> The mystic experience carries with it, in the words of William James, 'states of insight into depths of truth unplumbed by the discursive intellect'. The magician's passion is for knowledge; super-sensible knowledge but at the same time practical knowledge; For him the two need not be contradictory.[4]

Charles Tart, meanwhile, has subsumed mystical and magical states of mind within the categories of 'altered states' (ASC) which he differentiates from discrete ordinary states of consciousness that arise within the so-called 'consensus reality'. The latter is described as the domain of everyday communication and is supported by mutually agreed-upon concepts which underlie language and social behaviour. Tart's view of a state of consciousness implies 'an overall active organisation of consciousness, an interacting system of structures activated by attention/awareness energy.'[5]

Part of the shamanic process, as we have seen, involves a shifting of awareness away from the everyday context to an inner mental domain which acquires dominant reality as the shaman's consciousness pays increasing attention to symbolic images which arise. Tart's work involves an analysis of 'events in experiential space' and the range of activity between high rationality and high imagining ability. Normally in mystical states the latter is pronounced and the former is diminished. However, Tart has identified particular EEG patterns for out-of-the-body experiences which distinguish them from dream and mystical states, and has focused special attention on the so-called 'lucid dream'. In the lucid dream, the subject retains a degree of will and consciousness:

> One feels as rational and in control of one's mental state as in an ordinary state of consciousness, but one is still experientially located within the dream world. Here we have a range of rationality at a very high level and a range of ability to image also at a very high level.[6]

This category of altered states seems to fit closer than any other the phenomenon of shamanism. The shaman has vivid memory recall as a result of his visions. He is able to act purposively within his trance condition and is thus clearly distinguishable from the possessed medium who does not retain control of the altered state and frequently has no recollection of what has occurred. The shaman is also encountering a range of images which equate more closely with dream content than with the mystical practices of Zen and Yoga for which physiological tests have been made. In these cases the philosophical goal is a fusion with an undefined Absolute which transcends form and content.

Not surprisingly a distinctive EEG pattern has been found for
this condition; it is dominated by the alpha-wave cycle associated with relaxation and meditation and which produces high
amplitudes of 8–13 cycles per second.[7] However such primary
thought processes are not exclusively linked to alpha states and
can also embrace dream states and highly emotional mental
states ranging from very high to very low levels of cortical
arousal.[8] Although a complete range of tests has not been carried
out, we would clearly expect a different EEG result from a Zen
mystic meditating on the Void and a shaman undergoing a
dismemberment/rebirth process. The variance in belief systems
and the corresponding dissimilarities in perceptual content
appear to relate to different modes of consciousness, a point
raised by John Lilly, and which will be discussed subsequently.

Akira Kasamatsu and Tomai Hirai have reported the results
of an EEG study on Zen practitioners of the Soto and Rinzai
sects. It was found that during a Zen sitting (Zazen) alpha waves
were observed on the EEG monitoring equipment attached to
the scalps of the meditators after only fifty seconds. The ampli-
tude of these alpha waves continued and were subsequently
joined by a rhythmical theta train sometimes associated with
the hypnotic state. According to Kasamatsu and Hirai 'These . . .
stages of EEG changes were parallel with the disciples' mental
states which were evaluated by a Zen master.'[9]

Persistent alpha-wave activity was also reported by B. K.
Anand and his colleagues in their study of Yogis during *samadhi*
(meditative union) and also before and after meditation. It was
evident that two of the yogis with high pain thresholds were
able to retain high alpha even when their hands were exposed
to icy water (4° Centigrade) for up to fifty-five minutes. Two
others were able to actively eliminate the external bombardment
of strong light, loud auditory stimuli, vibration and heat,
without any influence on the alpha pattern.[10]

While these findings have no direct bearing on shamanism per
se they indicate the extent to which mystical practitioners can
shift their mode of attention and perceptual consciousness from
an external to an internal domain. In Tart's terminology they
transfer their consciousness energy from one experiential locale

to another. However, it is clear that aside from indicating such factors as alpha increase, EEG monitorings can tell us very little about the specific mental content of an altered state and nothing at all about such factors as symbolic transformation and archetypal journeys, which are quite crucial to the shamanic process. In the case of the shaman we are confronted with a trance phenomenon which as Ronald Shor indicates 'makes the distinction between reality and imagination progressively less relevant.'[11]

This aspect notwithstanding, interesting work on the left and right hemispheres of the brain has been undertaken by researchers like Robert Ornstein and David Galin.

Ornstein identifies different functional qualities in the left and right hemispheres of typical right-handed persons.[12] Among the aspects pertaining to the left hemisphere are: intellect, time and action, and explicit, analytic, propositional, lineal, sequential and verbal patterns. Among those pertaining to the right are the following: sensuous, timeless, receptive, tacit, gestalt, appositional, non-lineal, simultaneous and spatial qualities. Ornstein notes that meditation refers to a set of techniques which relate to what he calls 'personal' rather than 'intellectual' knowledge.

> As such, the exercises are designed to produce an alteration in consciousness – a shift away from the receptive and quiescent mode and visually a shift from an external focus of attention to an internal one . . . he attempts to keep all external sources of stimulation to a minimum to avoid being distracted from his object of meditation.[13]

Ornstein subsequently makes the point that on a comparative cultural basis, chanting, prayer, breath control and visualisation of symbols all play their part in meditation in helping shift the range of awareness.[14] It is significant that traditional mysticism, shamanism and contemporary trance magic share all of these aspects in common.

Alpha rhythms in the occipital cortex represent a state of decreased visual attention to the external environment and as we have seen are also found in Zen and Yogic meditation. This has led Ornstein to define meditation as a high-alpha state.

However he also notes that 'the esoteric psychologies' (which would include modern magical philosophy) seek a balance of intellectuality and intuition and 'the exercises usually stress the development of the receptive holistic mode'.[15]

It follows that irrespective of whether mysticism equates with high alpha in the sense that the mystic and magician alike are seeking union with a greater defined reality, they are indeed activating a holistic mode of consciousness, identified with the right hemisphere.[16] It is interesting however that several Golden Dawn members, among them the noted writers W.B. Yeats, Arthur Machen and Algernon Blackwood, found ritual magic a stimulus to the creative imagination. Yeats in particular accommodated a number of his Tarot trance meditations into his poems and the Tiphareth rebirth ritual into the recollections of Michael Robartes in 'Rosa Alchemica'.[17] The Tree of Life symbol in modern western magic is often interpreted so that Hod (intellect) is counterposed against Netzach (emotion, intuition) and the aim of the magician is to achieve a balanced rapport with the energies of his mythological unconscious.

David Galin emphasises that

the analytic and holistic modes are complementary; each provides a dimension which the other lacks. Artists, scientists, mathematicians, writing about their own creativity, all report that their work is based on a smooth integration of both modes.[18]

Consequently while mysticism is linked to right hemisphere activity it is likely that shamanism and trance magic – which brings purposeful activity to the altered state, as in the lucid dream – may combine right- and left-hemisphere activity.

MYTHOLOGICAL AND SYMBOLIC DOMAINS

The initial impetus in psychological research linking mythological symbols with the unconscious mind came from Carl Jung. Whereas Freud took the view that the unconscious contained and manifested infantile tendencies which had been repressed as 'incompatible', Jung regarded the unconscious psyche as embracing a much wider range of imagery. While for Freud the study of dreams was an important means of revealing neuroses, Jung regarded such dreams as a form of communication between the conscious and unconscious, expressing 'something specific that the unconscious was trying to say'.[19] He also noted that it was not appropriate to identify specific sexual motifs like the phallus or breast in dreams but to ask why specific images presented themselves. In this sense images came to have metaphysical meaning for him:

> A man may dream of inserting a key in a lock, of wielding a heavy stick, or of breaking down a door with a battering ram. Each of these can be regarded as a sexual allegory. But the fact that his unconscious, for its own purpose, has chosen one of these specific images – it may be the key, the stick or the battering ram – is also of major significance. The real task is to understand why the key has been preferred to the stick or the stick to the ram. And sometimes this might even lead one to discover that it is not the sexual act at all that is represented but some quite different point.[20]

Jung's study led him to the conclusion that such dreams were compensating for aspects of the personality which were unbalanced. He also believed that certain motifs derived from a level of the psyche which was universal, rather than derived from the individual ego. It was in the 'collective unconscious' that he discerned what he believed to be mythological processes. These were revealed in the form of 'religious images, their origin so far buried in the mystery of the past that they seem to have no human source.' He saw them as 'collective manifestations' emanating from primeval dreams and creative phantasies. 'As such,' he wrote, 'these images are involuntary spontaneous manifestations and by no means intentional inventions.'[21]

He also provided an example of how such a primordial image, or 'archetype' was formed:

> One   of   the   commonest   and   at   the   same   time   most

impressive experiences is the apparent movement of the
sun every day. We certainly cannot discover anything of
the kind in the unconscious, so far as known physical
process is concerned. What we do find, on the other hand,
is the myth of the sun hero in all its countless
modifications.[22]

Jung was also impressed by the fact that in dreams and visionary
states the archetype appeared to act independently of the
beholder:

The act of autonomy is such that psychologically, the spirit
manifests itself as a personal being, sometimes with
visionary clarity . . . in its strongest and most immediate
manifestations it displays a peculiar life of its own which
is felt as an independent being.[23]

While such views led many of Jung's colleagues to believe that
his study had passed from psychology into the realms of
mysticism, it is not surprising that such occultists as Dion
Fortune, Israel Regardie and W.E. Butler should have been
influenced by his approach. Jung's framework of unconscious
archetypes gave strength to the notion that the frameworks of
the Tree of Life presented a structure of archetypal deities which
could be influential in helping the magician harmonise and
balance his interior psychic processes. It also reinforced the
concept that such archetypes could take on individual status in
meditation and in the out-of-the-body or trance state, when
occultists undertook magical journeys and encountered god-
images direct. The magicians and Jung were agreed on the
impact that such an encounter could have. The latter wrote that
the archetype 'seizes hold of the psyche with a kind of primeval
force'.[24] The sheer impact of such a visionary experience was
regarded by the occultists of the Golden Dawn as initiatory, and
the sun hero referred to earlier as an example in Jung's writings,
was specifically the magician's goal in Tiphareth at the centre
of the Tree of Life: the visionary experience of spiritual renewal
associated mythologically with gods of life and light.

Several scholars influenced by Jung and writing from both

anthropological and psychological perspectives have further highlighted the links between mythology and consciousness. As we have noted, in the case of both the shaman, and the trance occultist following the symbolic paths of the Tarot upon the Tree of Life, the encountered mythological entities are seen as real and tangible in their presence. Indeed as James Hillman says, the images act upon the subject, bringing about a transformation:

> We learn from the alchemical psychologists to let the images work upon the experimenter; we learn to become the object of the work – even an object, or objectified image, of the imagination.[25]

In this sense the magician is moulded by the archetypal symbols of the psyche and is caught up in the ancestral drama which they present.

The links between the dream state and mythic consciousness have been delineated by Ira Progoff, James Hillman and Stanislav Grof, among others. Progoff, a depth psychologist with a marked Jungian orientation, believes that mythic states are best understood as belonging to the transpersonal level, that is to say, levels of consciousness beyond the usual domain of the ego. He writes:

> In general, dreams are that aspect of the symbolic dimension that is experienced in personal terms. When the symbolic dimension is perceived in transpersonal terms, in terms that pertain to more than the subjective experience of the individual reaching to what is universal in man, whether the experience is in sleeping or waking, myth is involved. It is myth because it touches what is ultimate in man and in his life, expresses it symbolically, and provides an inner perspective by which the mysteries of human existence are felt and entered into.[26]

Progoff rejects Freud's view that the unconscious contains only the repressed contents of the psyche and he has moved closer to Jung's model of the collective unconscious with its range of deep and universal archetypal images. However he also regards the unconscious as containing evolutionary potential for growth. As the 'seed of the personality' it contains 'the possibilities for future experience'.[27] The transpersonal domain also offers insights which only subsequently impinge upon the intellect.

Progoff's views show pronounced parallels with contemporary magical views of the psyche. As we have already indicated, occultists like Dion Fortune, W.E. Butler and Israel Regardie regard the magical journey as one which leads into the universally creative areas of the psyche, the very source of genius. The magician has before him, in terms of the Tree of Life framework, a complete matrix of mythological images which he can encounter in trance and incorporate into consciousness by means of magical identification. Contemporary ceremonial magic, with its emphasis on Tiphareth initiation, contains within its methodology an implicit aim to produce in each practitioner the god-man. Aleister Crowley wrote in 'Magick in Theory and Practice', 'The true God is man. In man are all things hidden.'[28] Both Progoff and Hillman stress that the transpersonal state which this implies transcends the function of intellect and precedes it. Hillman notes that we do not take intellect to the image: 'We sin against imagination whenever we ask our image for its meaning, requiring that images be translated into concepts.' By contrast, he notes 'Vision cannot be enacted unless archetypal persons strike us as utterly real'.[29]

In taking this position, Hillman is adopting essentially the same approach as the trance magician and shaman. The shift of awareness to the transpersonal, mythological domain produces a sequence of imaginal experiences which in a phenomenological sense are perceptually valid and totally convincing.

Stanislav Grof's 'Realms of the Human Unconscious' summarises his views of the unconscious mind as a result of seventeen years' research on LSD and other psychedelic drugs. As with Progoff, Grof pays special attention to transpersonal levels of consciousness which he divides into two divisions, those operating within the limits of 'objective reality' and those extending beyond it.

Within the first category (which embraces time/space extensions) Grof includes the out-of-the-body experience, which frequently occurs in LSD sessions:

> Some individuals have experienced themselves completely detached from their physical bodies, hovering above them or watching them from another part of the room. Occasionally the subject can also lose the awareness of the physical setting of the session and his consciousness moves into various experiential realms and subjective realities that appear to be entirely independent of material reality.[30]

However the physical perspective is capable of transforming into a mythological one. Grof gives as an illustration a subject who spent the first three hours of an LSD session experiencing a fantastic battle between the forces of light and darkness in the form of the confrontation of Ahura Mazda and Ahriman in the ancient Persian Zend Avesta. The subject later wrote:

> It was fought on all conceivable levels – in the cells and tissues of my body, on the surface of our planet throughout history, in the cosmos space and on a metaphysical, transcendental level.'[31]

Grof categorises such transpersonal experiences involving mythological and archetypal content as those 'beyond the framework of objective reality' and archetypal encounters are common during psychedelic sessions.

> An LSD subject can, for example, experience full identification with the archetypes of the Martyr, Fugitive, Outcast, Enlightened Ruler, Tyrant, Fool, Good Samaritan, Wise Old Man, Vicious Spoiler, Ascetic or Hermit. . . . In some of the most universal archetypes, the subject can identify with the roles of the Mother, Father, Child, Woman, Man or Lover. Many highly universalized roles are felt as sacred, as exemplified by the archetypes of the Great Mother, the Terrible Mother, the Earth Mother, Mother Nature, the Great Hermaphrodite or Cosmic Man.[32]

It is of considerable interest that several of these images are also present in the mythology of the Tarot, notably the Martyr (The

Hanged Man), The Enlightened Ruler (The Hierophant), The
Tyrant (The Charioteer, Death, The Devil), The Fool (The Fool),
The Wise Old Man (The Emperor), The Hermit (The Hermit),
The Great Mother (The Empress), The Terrible Mother (Justice),
The Earth Mother (Strength), and The Great Hermaphrodite
(The Fool, The Devil). It is appropriate to regard these as a series
of mythological encounters which the contemporary magician
experiences in his trance journey upon the Tree of Life.

Grof notes that several of his subjects have gravitated towards
mystical frameworks following their LSD sessions:

> some . . . have developed insights into entire systems of
> esoteric thought. Thus individuals unfamiliar with the
> Qabalah have had experiences described in the *Zohar* and
> *Sepher Yetzirah* and have demonstrated a surprising famili-
> arity with Qabalistic symbols. Others spontaneously
> played with the transcendental meaning of numbers and
> came to conclusions that were parallel with Pythagorean
> algebra or numerology. Subjects who had previously ridi-
> culed astrology and had a condescending attitude toward
> alchemy discovered deeper meaning in these systems and
> gained a deep appreciation of their metaphysical
> relevance.[33]

Quite aside from these observations on symbolic aspects of the
unconscious, we also find marked shamanic parallels in some
of the techniques of modern psychotherapy. Consequently it is
likely that some of the approaches currently employed in the
field of 'active imagination' will continue to throw light on the
perceptual universe of the shaman.

The skrying technique employed by the Golden Dawn
magicians and also the medieval occultist Edward Kelley seems
to resemble the half-dream state already referred to as the
'waking' or 'lucid' dream. The following account from an early
Freudian researcher is reminiscent of the observations of the
Tarot and Tattva meditators:

> In a dark room with eyes closed a definite scene will appear
> before me in apparently as bright an illumination as

daylight. I seem to be looking through my closed eyelids. The scene is apparently as real, as vivid, as detailed as an actual landscape. . . . Once the scene was a tropical landscape, with palm trees and a body of water. It was clear and detailed and appeared so real that I was surprised to find it unchanged by winking.[34]

The pioneering European psychotherapists evolved techniques of active imagination so that patients could visualise themselves in imaginal locations for therapeutic purposes. The psychotherapist learned

how to train the patient to relax, to separate his consciousness from its usual contents, to turn his awareness towards the movements of the imaginal; how to help him learn to enter into his imaginary body, to insert himself into the imaginary scene, to move within it, to encounter threatening images and to allow affect to rise, how to recognise and work with resistances; how or whether to interpret and analyse the waking dream; how to see the patient's experience in the imaginal realm in relaxation to other aspects of his existence.[35]

Relaxation of the body and willed imagination involving a shift of consciousness to a distinct visualised form are basic magical techniques for producing the out-of-the-body condition known by occultists as astral projection. When this dissociational state is linked to a meditative symbol the trance domain acquires distinctive mythological qualities, as in the case of the visionary Tattva and Tarot projections that have already been discussed. Interestingly, some psychotherapists have employed techniques of active imagination which resemble shamanic descent and ascent.

Eugene Caslant in a darkened consulting room taught his patients to ascend and descend from one imaginary level to another by evoking such images as the ladder, the staircase and the flying chariot. The subject imagined himself placed on and venturing into interior imaginary space:

ascension not only brought about an inner feeling of elevation but also markedly affected the nature of the vision . . . higher levels were usually associated with more pleasant affect than lower ones.[36]

Robert Desoille, a student of Caslant's, used to encourage his patients to enter imaginary archetypal locations (an ocean, cave or encounter with a mythical beast and so on) until the anxiety aroused by the images in these situations simply drained away. He believed, with Caslant, that ascension was associated with warmth, slower respiration and heartbeat, sensations of light and euphoria, and more 'positive' imagery.

In a comparable manner the trance magicians' ascent upon the Tree of Life or journeys to archetypal domains tend to produce transcendental images of a pure and integrative nature. Descent indicates a mythological aspiration towards a lower evolutionary stage than man (e.g. the animal man) and the visions of such magicians tend to have a retrogressive quality. As we have noted, the occult artist, Austin Spare, evolved a unique technique of inducing the trance state by means of concentrating on magical sigils and believed that in trance he could enter animal forms which had been his own earlier incarnations. By retracing this succession of 'personalities' Spare thought he could arrive at his 'first form' and then leap into the undifferentiated void of universal consciousness which he named Kia. His visionary style of graphic art became increasingly dominated by half-human and half-animal forms (satyrs, horned beings) and distinctly atavistic in nature.[37]

Leuner's technique of psychotherapy, by comparison, was not far removed from Spare's perspective but lacked the obsessive and retrogressive direction of the trance artist. Leuner's process involved confronting the symbolic vision and any antagonistic forms like the snake or bear which might arise:

The patient is encouraged neither to escape nor to struggle. Instead he is instructed to stay put and watch, for example, the animal. He should notice and describe any detail. By staring at the animal the patient's feelings not only become neutralized but there is an opportunity created by which to discover the message or meaning which the creature's existence conveys. The frightening animal may become weaker and smaller and it may sooner or later be transformed into another creature – a less frightening and often a benign one. Psychoanalytically, the end result of successful confrontation is a strengthening of the ego. The ego confronts the imagination and in a variety of ways is taught to overcome it.[38]

In both traditional shamanic accounts and also in records of occult trance journeys, as we have seen, transformatory images and the presence of hostile creatures or situations are common. The shaman often expects to undergo ritual ordeals and ward off potentially hostile influences before he reaches the domain of the deity he is seeking. Similarly images in the Tarot mythology such as Death and The Devil are distinctly illusory and challenge the magician's sense of certainty. The technique of the magician or shaman is invariably to allow himself to undergo the transformational process which frequently involves dismemberment and renewal, and not to panic when confronted with an experiential crisis.

Wolfgang Kretschmer's techniques of psychotherapy also have pronounced shamanic aspects. Kretschmer's approach has been to take his patient through symbolic imaginal situations which relate to specific functions within the psyche. In meditation the patient journeys:

(a) through a meadow covered with fresh grass and flowers
(b) slowly up the side of a mountain
(c) through a grove into a chapel.

Kretschmer notes that when the subject reaches a state of deep meditation these locales move from an 'everyday' aspect into a symbolic context:

As the meditator returns to the meadow he does not experience things as he would in the ordinary world. Rather the meadow provides a symbol of the hypnotic level of consciousness and stimulates the emotions on this level. The individual takes an ordinary situation as the

means of experiencing the primordial content of the
symbol of the meadow.

This in turn may lead to an experience of the meadow as Mother
Nature or the 'blossoming of life', and can be contrasted with
the obverse image of a forest inhabited by demons. Kretschmer
believes that the way in which the subject visualises his meadow
demonstrates aspects of his psychic condition.[39]

The meditation based on ascent up the side of a mountain is
of special interest. Not only does it mirror a major shamanic
theme but the same experience is symbolised in the Tarot path
of The Hermit, in which the magician journeys in isolation
slowly upwards to the loftier reaches of the Tree of Life.

As in the case of the shaman, Kretschmer notes that in
climbing the mountain

> the meditator will generally symbolise some obstacle in his
> way so that he must prove himself . . . climbing is a symbol
> of a movement during which man demonstrates his
> capacity to develop toward the goal of psychic freedom,
> the peak of human being. The passage through the forest
> on the way up the mountain gives the meditator the oppor-
> tunity to reconcile himself with the dark, fearful side of
> nature.[40]

Kretschmer's symbol of the chapel, meanwhile, has an apparent
parallel in the shaman's cave or the magician's temple; it is the
location of the sacred mystery itself. As detailed earlier, in the
initiation of Tiphareth, the Hermetic magician comes forth from
the tomb of Christian Rosenkreuz and the theme of spiritual
renewal is inherent.

During the meditation, according to Kretschmer, 'subli-
mations' may occur. By this he means 'transformation, spiritual-
ization or humanization',[41] and once again we find a comparable
situation with the shaman who gains new magical powers and
self-esteem after his journey or the trance occultist who is
'initiated' as a result of his contact with transpersonal
archetypes.

EXPLANATIONS OF MYSTICAL STATES

Two main theories have evolved to account for mystical experiences. The first of these, formulated by Raymond Prince, takes the position that such experiences are 'regressions in the service of the ego'. The second, associated with the work of Arthur Deikman, describes them as 'deautomatizations of ego functions'.

Prince's regression theory holds that mystical states occur when an individual or group is confronted with a problem which would normally be insoluble by normal means. The individual's ego regresses in order to discover a simple solution to a complex situation. Prince finds a parallel here with mystical claims of union with the cosmos, and the sense of well-being. He regards such mystical experience 'as a flash-back to the time when the self and other are not differentiated, a reunification with the mother's breast.'[42]

Deikman, on the other hand, takes the view that the mystic's process of meditation invests attention energy in activities which have become automatic and thus returns them to awareness. New perceptions therefore have increased sensory intensity and richness. The quality of the mystical experience hinges on the nature of the focusing stimulus:

> The control of the mystic experience reflects not only its unusual mode of consciousness but also the particular stimuli being processed through that mode. The mystic experience can be beatific, satanic, revelatory or psychotic, depending on the stimuli predominant in each case. . . . The available scientific evidence tends to support the view that the mystic experience is one of internal perception, an experience that can be ecstatic, profound, or therapeutic for purely internal reasons.[43]

Deikman's theory would seem to throw more light on the shamanic experience than Prince's. Prince emphasises devotional forms of mysticism in which love and contemplation are foremost within the belief structure and the resulting sensation of 'one-ness' is invariably described by believers in subjective and simplistic terms which in some measure justify his conclusion. However, there is very much less security in the shaman's mystical quest. He faces dismemberment and transformation and gains magical powers only after ritual ordeals. In the case of the trance occultist using the Tarot mythology as his framework, the ultimate experience at the top of the Tree is represented by the image of the Hermaphrodite (symbolising the union of sexual polarity) who steps from the peak of the mountain into the Void of total dissolution. The image of the Great Mother, on the other hand, is represented lower on the Tree in the form of The Empress.

Deikman's theory is supported by the fact that trance occultists have visionary experiences which derive explicitly from the symbol they focus on, whether it is a Tattva, Tarot card, Enochian square, or some comparable path-working symbol. As Deikman indicates, the experience can take a variety of forms and these reflect the inner psychic condition of the person concerned.

Interesting additional material is outlined by Ronald Siegel in a recent article on hallucinations.[44] He notes that hallucinations 'may be induced by emotional and other factors such as drugs, alcohol and stress, and may occur in any of the senses.' Heinrich Kluver undertook a series of experiments at the University of Chicago in 1926 with the peyote cactus Lophophora Williamsii, which is also associated with shamanic practice among the Huichols and Tarahumares. The psychedelic imagery reported included grating/lattice/fretwork patterns; cobwebs, tunnels, funnels and alleys, and also spirals.

Siegel notes, 'During the peak hallucinatory periods the subjects frequently described themselves as having become part of the imagery. At such times they stopped using similes in their reports and asserted that the images were real. . . .' The subjects frequently reported feeling dissociated from their bodies. Siegel comes to the same conclusion as Deikman, namely that the experiences are the result of internal processes: 'Hallucinations are stored images in the brain.'[45]

We have already found the themes of dissociation and alternative experiential realities in both shamanism and modern trance magic. As Deikman, Ornstein, Hillman, Tart and Grof have indicated, the crucial factor seems to be the way in which attention is brought to bear in the altered state of consciousness. Shamanism seems to involve techniques of channelling consciousness towards profoundly transpersonal regions of the psyche and the visionary experiences which result are shaped by cultural factors; these also provide the context and the 'stimulus' for the trance journey in the first instance.

An important consideration then is the degree to which the given belief system of the trance magician operates in the altered state. Interesting insights into this process are provided by the well-known neurophysiologist John Lilly who undertook a series of sensory deprivation experiments in a specially prepared tank at the Institute of Mental Health in Bethesda, Maryland.[46] Floating with a special breathing apparatus in water at body temperature, and in an environment of solitude and darkness, Lilly experienced gravity-free effects and heightened inner awareness. He writes:

> I went through dream-like states, trance-like states, mystical states. In all of these states I was totally intact.[47]

Lilly also took LSD–25 in a supportive environment with a colleague and discovered that the religious conditioning of his youth manifested itself in a visionary form. He experienced the ecstatic flight of the soul, saw angelic beings and encountered an aged, patriarchal God seated in his throne:

> I moved with the music into Heaven. I saw God on a tall throne as a giant, wise, ancient Man. He was surrounded by angel choruses, cherubim, and seraphim, the saints were moving by his throne in a stately procession. I was there in Heaven, worshipping God, worshipping the angels, worshipping the saints in full and complete transport of religious ecstasy.[48]

In Lilly's view, visionary experiences of this kind are a direct manifestation of belief-programming fed as a result of cultural patterns into 'the human biocomputer'. Beliefs can be inhibiting in the altered state or they can be revelatory.

Between 1970–1 John Lilly studied with Oscar Ichazo, a Chilean mystic based in Arica, Chile, and evolved a structure which he believed expressed the consciousness levels of some of the major religions. Following Ichazo's system which in turn derived from the Russian teacher George Gurdjieff, Lilly divided potential human consciousness into vibrational levels, ranging from the deeply depressed and 'evil' state to a transcendental state of union with 'universal mind'. He also identified the more positive levels with the Hindu chakras, or inner energy centres aligned vertically in the body. 'Christ-consciousness' he located over the heart, identifying it with love and grace within a social and physical context, while Buddha consciousness was located in the head and identified with mystical clairvoyant faculties. Lilly described the supreme mental state as 'classical Sartori' – fusion with God/mind/energy and the Void. What Lilly outlined in this framework was very comparable to what magicians have traditionally portrayed in their macrocosmic/microcosmic models, namely that man in a metaphorical sense contains the whole universe. Full mystical realisation produces total man, the archetype known to Qabalists as Adam Kadmon. The god-man, represented here by Christ is identified with the central but 'half-way' stage of the heart, while full cosmic consciousness has no symbolic correlates and is a totally ineffable state of transcendental, spiritual knowledge.

Lilly's views constitute in some respects yet another brand of mysticism, and accordingly would seem to fall outside the domain of empirical enquiry. However, it is of considerable interest that the Zen and Yogic practitioners whose EEG readings were taken during meditation sessions were endeavouring to attain Sartori/Samadhi states of awareness. Thus, to some degree, we are now able to correlate mystical levels of consciousness with physiological brain-wave patterns; we are not solely dependent on subjective reports of the visionary experience. Also, Lilly's framework develops the idea that different religious beliefs produce different 'consciousness effects' in their devotees and implies that culturally related symbolic levels of religious perception are more significant than Jung's quest for inherent archetypes. Lilly stresses the ingredients within a 'programme of belief' since these will actually manifest as real in the altered state of consciousness. If the content of belief, such as the shamanic expectation of transformation is culturally reinforced it becomes an experiential reality in the trance state. Lilly's position complements Deikman's point that the stimulus (or belief input) has a direct bearing on the quality and impact of the mystical experience. Claude Lévi-Strauss also emphasises the interrelation of belief and consciousness, and the cultural framework from which they derive:

> myths signify the mind that evolves them by making use of the world of which it is itself a part. Thus there is a simultaneous production of the myths themselves by the mind that generates them and, by the myths, of an image of the world which is already inherent in the structure of the mind.[49]

APPENDIX B
Major 'Mythological Correspondence' in Western Magic

Major 'Mythological Correspondences' in Western Magic

	QABALAH	GREEK	ROMAN	EGYPTIAN
Origen	Kether (Eheieh)	Kronos	Saturn	Ptah (Memphis) Atum-Ra (Heliopolis) Amon (Thebes)
Father	Chokmah (Jehovah)			Thoth
Mother	Binah (Jehovah, Elohim)	Rhea	Rhea	Isis
Demiurge (Intermediary God-Figure)	Chesed (El)	Zeus (Hera, Demeter) Poseidon (Amphritrite)	Jupiter (Juno) Neptune (Amphitrite)	Ra
	Geburah (Elohim Gebor)	Ares	Mars	Herus (Warrior)
Son	Tiphareth (Jehovah Aloah Va Daath)	Helios-Apollo, Dionysus	Apollo	Osiris
	Netzach (Jehovah Tzabaoth)	Aphrodite	Venus	Hathor
	Hod (Elohim Tzabaoth)	Hermes	Mercury	Anubis
	Yesod (Shaddai El Chai)	Hecate, Artemis	Diana	Bast
Daughter	Malkuth (Adonai Ha-Aretz)	Persephone	Proserpine	Geb

APPENDIX C
Organisations and Groups

The following are contact addresses for groups mentioned in this book, specialising in magical or shamanic activity:

MAGIC

The DOME Foundation:
    217 W. San Francisco,
    Santa Fe,
    New Mexico 87501, USA.
Servants of the Light (SOL):
    PO Box 215, St Helier,
    Jersey, The Channel Islands.
Magus Phantasy Group:
    PO Box 321,
    GPO Sydney, 2001 Australia.

SHAMANISM

The Center for Shamanic Studies:
    Box 673,
    Belden Station,
    Norwalk,
    Connecticut 06852, USA.

Human Dimensions West Institute:
    PO Box 5037,
    Ojai,
    California, USA.

Notes

CHAPTER 1 THE WORLD OF THE SHAMAN

1   M. Eliade, 'Shamanism', p. 5.
2   C. Blacker, 'The Catalpa Bow', p. 204.
3   Ibid., p. 207.
4   M. Harner, 'The Jivaro', p. 154.
5   A. P. Elkin, 'Aboriginal Men of High Degree' (2nd edn), p. 82.
6   Ibid., pp. 84–5.
7   Henry Munn, in M. Harner (ed.), 'Hallucinogens and Shamanism', p. 100.
8   It is evident that for the Mazatecs the Christian pantheon has been included so that Jesus and the Virgin Mary have magical healing power. Shamanic appeals to this power may therefore be expected to prove efficacious. A similar pattern is found in the Coptic codex translated by occultist Florence Farr under the heading 'Egyptian Magic'. The Ethiopian Gnostics regarded Jesus as a magical authority having access to the supreme and most profound domains of the cosmos. Accordingly they sought his secret initiatory names so that they might have access to his source of spiritual power. See also N. Drury, 'The Path of the Chameleon'.
9   G. Reichel-Dolmatoff in M. Harner (ed.), 'Hallucinogens and Shamanism', p. 166.
10 G. Vasilevich, Early concepts about the universe among the Evenks, in H. N. Michael (ed.), 'Studies in Siberian Shamnism', p. 74.
11 Ibid., p. 72.
12 A. F. Anisimov, Cosmological concepts of the people of the north, in H. N. Michael (ed.), op. cit., p. 161.
13 Ibid., p. 161.

14 It is important to note that such conjurings should not be considered merely delusory. They are regarded as a tangible manifestation of intangible causality. A. P. Elkin notes that even when sleight of hand occurs in an Aboriginal healing session it seems to be necessary to show physically that a magical cure has been effected (Ekin, op. cit., p. 7).

15 Vasilevich, op. cit., p. 59.

16 Eliade, op. cit., p. 120.

17 Ibid., p. 265.

18 Blacker, op. cit. p. 23.

19 Eliade, op. cit., p. 147.

20 S. Larsen, 'The Shaman's Doorway', p. 70.

21 B. M. Du Toit (ed.), 'Drugs, Rituals and Altered States of Consciousness', p. 19. The spirit world of the voudou becomes a very real one. A. Metraux, 'Voodoo in Haiti', p. 215, provides details of a marriage certificate recording the mystical union of a woman and her spirit.

22 G. M. Weil (ed.), 'The Psychedelic Reader', p. 90.

23 The following is a brief summary of the main effects of these hallucinogens:

Banisteriopsis

The common ingredient of yage, caapi and ayahuasca is Banisteriopsis, which in turn contains the alkaloids harmine, harmaline and d-tetrahydroharmine. 'Typically, Banisteriopsis is taken by South American Indian shamans of the tropical forest in order to perceive the supernatural world and to contact and to affect the behaviour of supernatural entities . . .' (Harner, op. cit., p. 5).

He also summarises as the main themes associated with the drug culturally: (a) the sensation of separation of the 'soul' and the physical body, (b) visions of predatory animals, (c) contact with the supernatural and heaven and hell states, (d) visions of distant locations and persons and (e) explanatory visions of events such as thefts and mysterious homicides (pp. 172–3). However, several of these may be linked. The so-called-out-of-the-body experience is associated with the sensation of flight, but can also produce visionary and symbolic experiences (see R. Monroe, 'Journeys Out of the Body' and related literature listed in the Bibliography).

Datura

Datura is a solanaceous genus with two main herbaceous species *D. meteloides* and *D. inoxia*, both of which are associated with magical use. Usually the pulverised seeds of Datura are dropped into native beers and consumed in this fashion. The intoxication is frequently followed by a deep sleep during which vivid hallucinations arise. Shamans, for example among the Jivaro, use the experience to diagnose disease and to divine theft. In Mexico the Datura species are collectively known as Toloache and in the American south west, *D. meteloides* is referred to as Jimson Weed. The primary active substance in the plant is scopolamine, a drug in the same class of chemicals as cocaine and atropine although its effects are different. Scopolamine dries out the mucous membrane areas in the nose, mouth and throat and in moderate to large intakes may produce hallucinations lasting up to three days. These hallucinations are auditory as often as visual and may often result in the subject holding conversations with imaginary beings.

Mescal beans

Unrelated to the 'mescal button' of the peyote cactus (*Lophophora Williamsii*), so called mescal beans, are the dark red seeds of the shrub *Sophora secundiflora*, and their hallucinatory effects derive from cytisine, a highly poisonous crystalline alkaloid which can produce nausea and death from respiratory failure. It was used extensively by the Plains Indians to induce initiatory visions in the 'Red Bean Dance', and also had a divinatory function, but its cultural use has diminished in recent times. It is still present among the Kiowa and Comanche Indians, but only in a ceremonial capacity. Mescal beans were to a large extent replaced as a narcotic by the more spectacular but less dangerous peyote cactus.

Morning Glory

Morning Glory, or *Ololiuhqui* as it is known in Mexico, is the seed of a vine, which for some time was confused with Datura. It is now known that only two of the numerous species of Morning Glory are hallucinogenically active: *Rivea corymbosa* (with a blue/violet flower). If the seeds are swallowed, they produce no effect on the body, but if crushed or powdered may produce hallucinations similar to those associated with LSD, but of a shorter duration. Bright colours and patterns may be observed and also the sense of perceiving objects from a distance. In 1960 Albert Hofmann identified the active constituents as the amides of lysergic acid and of d-lysergic acid, chanoclavine and clymoclavine, substances also found in the ergot fungus (Claviceps purpurea) and thus directly linked to chemically synthesised LSD.

Peyete cactus

Known as *Lophophora Williamsii*, Peyote is especially associated with the Huichol Indians, who conduct a ritual hunt for this sacred plant after the rainy season in the early spring. In Peyote ceremonies Indians would normally consume between four and twenty 'buttons', invariably during the night time and not by day. Initially the Peyote causes nausea and vomiting, but around an hour later, exhilarating effects occur. Colour and sound are intensified, and there are sensory hallucinations and also heightened awareness and perception. After 3–4 hours, the sense of visual excitement is usually replaced by inner retrospection and after 8–10 hours, the subject becomes very tired and invariably falls asleep. According to Schultes, Peyote is not addictive (R. E. Schultes, Botanical sources of New World narcotics, in Weil, op. cit., p. 101). It contains eight isoquinoline alkaloids, one of which – Mescalin – produces vivid hallucinations.

Psilocybe Mexicana

A major narcotic mushroom especially found in Oaxaca, Psilocybe Mexicana was investigated by Albert Hofmann and R. G. Wasson, who discovered it being used for spiritual healing by a Mazatec curandera named Maria Sabina. The mushroom is also used by Mazatec sorcerers and according to Henry Munn (M. Harner (ed.), 'Hallucinogens and Shamanism', p. 88) produces inspired language in those who consume it. The mushroom intoxication produces heightened awareness of supernatural entities such as the 'laa' (Mazatec fairies), but also vivid and colourful hallucinations. Initial muscular relaxation may be followed by hilarity and then hallucinations – which may be both visual and auditory – ensue. The subject may feel isolated and indifferent to his environment, which becomes increasingly unreal to him. His visionary state presents, on the other hand, a more captivating 'reality'. Psilocybine was synthesised from the mushroom by Hofmann and is now being clinically analysed as a possible aid to psychiatry and therapy.

24 Harner, 'Hallucinogens and Shamanism', p. 155.
25 Ibid., p. 167.
26 P. Furst (ed.), 'Flesh of Gods', p. 93.
27 Ibid., p. 103.
28 The word 'phasmata' is used by Plato in 'Phaedrus'.
29 R. G. Wasson, 'The Road to Eleusis', p. 37.
30 Ibid., p. 37.
31 Ibid., p. 47. In a recent article, ergotism has also been proposed as a possible factor in the Salem witchcraft crisis of 1692 (Linda R. Caporael, Ergotism: the Satan loosed in Salem?, in 'Science', vol. 192): several subjects who may have been victims of ergot poisoning in rye, experienced symptoms linked to convulsive ergotism, in particular the experience of hallucinations and visions of spectral beings. One victim reported an encounter with an entity whose features resembled a monkey with a cock's feet but with the face of a man ('the thing spoke to me . . .'). Others reported witch-like familiars. Accounts of perceptual disturbances, tingling sensations in the skin, convulsions and muscular contractions were widespread at the trials. Caporael indicates that environmental factors undoubtedly influenced the nature of the hallucinations. What is of special interest in comparing the Salem witchcraft incidents with Eleusian mysteries is that the spectres enountered in the hallucinatory state were apparently regarded in both instances as totally real.
31 In his first book, 'The Teachings of Don Juan', Carlos Castaneda describes spectacular transformation into bird form under hallucinogenic influence. Having smoked a dried mushroom mixture (Psilocybe Mexicana), he was able to transform his perceptions so that his head became the body of a crow. Legs extended from his chin and wings emerged from his cheeks. He experienced the weightlessness of aerial flight often associated with traditional shamanism (ibid., p. 189). This experience is remarkably similar to that of the Greek shaman, Aristeas of Proconnesus, although as far as we are aware, hallucinogens were not involved in the latter case.
32 Drury, 'The Path of the Chameleon', p. 113.

CHAPTER 2 SHAMANIC TRANCE

1 A. Bharati (ed.), 'The Realm of the Extra-Human', p. 316.
2 C. Blacker, 'The Catalpa Bow', p. 23.
3 B. M. Du Toit (ed.), 'Drugs, Rituals and Altered States of Consciousness', p. 9.
4 C. M. Edsman (ed.), 'Studies in Shamanism', p. 76.
5 I. Lewis, 'Ecstatic Reigion', p. 180.
6 M. Eliade, 'Shamanism', p. 29.
7 Quoted in Eliade, op. cit., p. 31.
8 E. Arbman, 'Ecstasy or Religious Trance', p. 297.
9 Eliade, op. cit., p. 29.
10 E. De Martino, 'Magic, Primitive and Modern', p. 132. quoting Rasmussen's diaries: K. Rasmussen, A shaman's journey to the sea spirit, in W. Lessa and E. Vogt (eds), 'Reader in Comparative Religion'.
11 Edsman, op. cit., p. 174.
12 Ibid., p. 26.
13 Rasmussen, op. cit., in Lessa and Vogt (eds), op. cit., p. 390.
14 Lessa and Vogt (eds), op. cit., p. 390.
15 Blacker, op. cit., p. 195.
16 Eliade, op. cit., p. 88.
17 G. Vasilevich, Early concepts about the universe among the Evenks, in H. N. Michael (ed.), 'Studies in Siberian Shamanism', p. 58.
18 A. F. Anisimov, Cosmological concepts of the people of the north, in H. N. Michael, op. cit., p. 186.
19 Eliade, op. cit., p. 120.
20 Ibid., p. 40.
21 Ibid., p. 88.
22 A. P. Elkin, 'Aboriginal Men of High Degree' (2nd edn), p. 20.
23 Ibid., pp. 142–3.
24 Ibid., p. 143.
25 S. Larsen, 'The Shaman's Doorway', p. 195.

CHAPTER 3 MAGICAL SYMBOLS AND CEREMONIAL

1 See Appendix B for examples of these mythological correspondences.
2 I. Regardie, 'The Tree of Life', p. 106.

3 F. Bardon, 'The Practice of Magical Evocation', p. 20.
4 E. Levi, 'The Key of the mysteries', p. 174.
5 E. A. Wallis Budge (ed.), 'The Bandlet of Righteousness', p. 3.
6 Ibid., p. 4.
7 Ibid., p. 5.
8 Temura is a traditional Qabalistic technique of changing the position of letters in a word to create a new word which relates in symbolic meaning to the original. It was often used to veil secret Qabalistic names, particularly those related to God. God names that are Temura equivalents show different aspects of the same transcendental reality.
9 A. Crowley, 'Book Four', p. 42.
10 D. Fortune, 'Applied Magic', pp. 56–7.
11 Crowley, 'Book Four', p. 46.
12 For examples see the list of Jewish god-names in Appendix B.
13 Crowley, 'Book Four', p. 23.
14 Ibid., p. 122.
15 'The Book of Enoch' and early forms of Merkabah mysticism provide a cosmology based on thrones and a series of mystical emanations from the godhead. See Gershom Scholem, 'Major Trends in Jewish Mysticism'.

CHAPTER 4 TECHNIQUES OF MAGICAL TRANCE

1 F. King (ed.), 'Astral projection, magic and alchemy', pp. 73–4.
2 Celia Green reports in her survey, 'Out of the Body Experiences', that the existence of a cord, perceived as connecting the 'astral body' and the physical one, was not often reported by subjects claiming projection. Only 3.5 per cent felt connected in this way (p. 122). In an Australian survey of 200 subjects, Peter Bicknell found only 1 per cent making this claim (N. Drury and G. G. Tillett, 'Other Temples, Other Gods', p. 161).
3 King, op. cit.
4 Ibid., p. 69.
5 N. Drury, 'Don Juan, Mescalito and Modern Magic', p. 37.
6 King, op. cit., p. 82.
7 Yod is the sacred first letter of the Qabalistic Name of God JHVH.
8 King, op. cit., pp. 82–4.
9 See Israel Regardie's introduction to Aleister Crowley's 'The Vision and the Voice'.
10 Crowley, 'The Vision and the Voice', pp. 57–8.

11 Ibid., p– 61.
12 Ibid., pp. 61–2.
13 Ibid., pp. 199–201.
14 Ibid., p. 199.
15 Ibid., p. 201.
16 G. Knight, 'A Practical Guide to Qabalistic Symbolism', vol. 2, pp. 66–7.
17 See Joan Halifax, 'Shamanic Voices'.
18 Knight, op. cit., vol. 2, p. 115.
19 P. Case, 'The Tarot', p. 123.
20 King, op. cit., p. 66.
21 Ibid., p. 67.
22 Specific allusions to Golden Dawn 'inner plane' orders of ritual attainment.
23 King, op. cit., pp. 58–9.

CHAPTER 5 NEW DIRECTIONS: FROM ATAVISTIC RESURGENCE TO THE INNER LIGHT

1 According to Kenneth Grant, Spare joined the Argenteum Astrum on 10 July 1910 (K. Grant, 'Images and Oracles of Austin Osman Spare', p. 7).
2 A. Spare, 'The Book of Pleasure', p. 47.
3 K. Grant, quoted in N. Drury and S. Skinner, 'The Search for Abraxas', p. 66.
4 Spare, 'The Book of Pleasure', p. 53.
5 K. Grant, 'The Magical Revival', p. 188.
6 K. Grant, 'Images and Oracles of Austin Osman Spare', p. 73.
7 Grant, 'The Magical Revival', p. 201.
8 Grant, 'Images and Oracles of Austin Osman Spare', p. 33.
9 Ibid., p. 44.
10 A. Spare, 'Focus on Life', p. 35.
11 Ibid.
12 E. Steinbrecher, 'The Guide Meditation', p. 30.
13 Ibid., p. 48.
14 Ibid., p. 69.
15 Ibid., pp. 54–5.
16 Ibid., p. 58.
17 'F.P.D.', 'The Old Religion', in Basil Wilby (ed.), 'New Dimensions Red Book'.
18 Ibd18   Ibid., p. 47.

19 Ibid., p. 49.
20 Ibid., p. 78.
21 D. Ashcroft-Nowicki, Highways of the mind, in 'Round Merlin's Table', no. 50, pp. 14–15.
22 'Round Merlin's Table', no. 53, pp. 5–6.

POSTSCRIPT: WHY THE SHAMAN?

1 J. Campbell (ed.), 'Myths, Dreams and Religion', p. 114.

APPENDIX: SHAMANISM, MAGIC AND THE STUDY OF CONSCIOUSNESS

1 J. H. Leuba, 'Psychology of Religious Mysticism', p. 1.
2 E. Underhill, 'Mysticism', p. 97.
3 J. Ehrenwald, 'The ESP Experience', p. 159.
4 H. Whitehead, Reasonably fantastic: some perspectives on scientology, science fiction, and occultism, in I. Zaretsky and M. Leone (eds), 'Religious Movements in Contemporary America', p. 564.
5 P. Lee, 'Symposium on Consciousness', p. 91.
6 Ibid., p. 114.
7 The normally accepted division of brain activity is as follows:
    Alpha waves have a frequency around 8–13 cycles per second and indicate a state of deep concentration.
    Beta waves occur in alert, waking consciousness and measure around 13 cycles per second.
    Theta waves are associated with drowsiness and the state immediately preceding sleep. They measure around 4–7 cycles per second.
    Delta waves are produced in deep sleep and measure around 0–4 cycles per second.
    Some psychologists, among them R. E. Ornstein, have linked mystical mediation closely to the alpha range.
8 C. Martindale, What makes creative people different, in P. Whitten, 'Being Human Today – Psychological Perspectives', p. 46.
9 C. Tart (ed.), 'Altered States of Consciousness', p. 501.
10 Ibid., pp. 503–4.
11 Ibid., p. 248.
12 R. E. Ornstein, 'The Psychology of Consciousness', p. 47.

13 Ibid., pp. 123–4.
14 Ibid., p. 139.
15 Ibid., p. 165.
16 Lee, op. cit., p. 23.
17 W. Yeats, 'Mythologies', p. 288.
18 Lee, op. cit., p. 40.
19 C. Jung, 'Man and His Symbols', p. 12.
20 Ibid., p. 13.
21 Ibid., pp. 41–2.
22 C. Jung, 'Two Essays on Analytical Psychology', p. 68.
23 See C. Jung, 'Spirit and life' (1926), reprinted in 'The Structure and Dynamics of the Psyche'.
24 Jung, 'Two Essays', pp. 65–6.
25 J. Hillman, 'Revisioning Psychology', p. 40.
26 J. Campbell (ed.), 'Myths, Dreams and Religion', p. 177.
27 Ibid., p. 181.
28 A. Crowley, 'Magick in Theory and Practice', p. 153.
29 Hillman, op. cit., pp. 39, 42.
30 S. Grof, 'Realms of Unconscious', p. 186.
31 Ibid., p. 187.
32 Ibid., p. 198.
33 Ibid., p. 201.
34 M. Watkins, 'Waking Dreams', p. 52.
35 Ibid.
36 Ibid., p. 58.
37 N. Drury and S. Skinner, 'The Search for Abraxas', pp. 49–71.
38 Watkins, op. cit., p. 66.
39 Tart, 'Altered States of Consciousness', p. 221.
40 Ibid., p. 222.
41 Ibid.
42 I. Zaretsky and M. Leone (eds), op. cit., p. 257.
43 Tart, 'Altered States of Consciousness', p. 43.
44 R. Siegel, Hallucinations, 'Scientific American', October 1977, pp. 132, 140.
45 Ibid., p. 140.
46 J. Lilly, 'The Centre of the Cyclone', p. 75.
47 Ibid., 1 pp. 52–3.
48 Ibid., p. 25.
49 C. Lévi-Strauss, 'The Raw and the Cooked', p. 341.

Bibliography

Aaronson, B. and Osmond, H. (eds), 'Psychedelics', Doubleday/Anchor, New York, 1970.

Anand, B. K., Some aspects of electroencephalograph studies in Yogis, in C. Tart (ed.), 'Altered States of Consciousness', Wiley, New York, 1969.

Arban, E., 'Ecstasy or Religious Trance', vol. 1, Uppsala, 1963.

Balikci, A., Shamanistic behaviour among the Netsilik Eskimos, in J. Middleton (ed.), 'Magic, Witchcraft and Curing', The Natural History Press, New York, 1967.

Bardon, F., 'Initiation into Hermetics', Osiros Verlag, Koblenz, 1962.

Bardon, F., 'The Practice of Magical Evocation', Rudolf Pravica, Graz, 1967.

Barron, F., Hallucinogenic Drugs, in J. L. M. McGaugh (ed.), 'Psychology: Readings From Scientific American', 19.

Basilov, V., Shamanism in Central Asia, in A. Bharati (ed.), 'The Realm of Extra-Human', Mouton, The Hague, 1976.

Belo, J., 'Trance in Bali', Greenwood Press, 1977.

Bharati, A. (ed.), 'The Realm of the Extra-Human', Mouton, The Hague, 1976.

Blacker, C., 'The Catalpa Bow', Allen & Unwin, London, 1975.

Bourguignon, E., Cross-cultural perspectives on the religious uses of altered states of consciousness, in I. Zaretsky and M. Leone (eds), 'Religious Movements in Contemporary America', Princeton University Press, 1974.

Bourguignon, E., 'Possession', Chandler & Sharp, San Francisco, 1976.

Budge Wallis, E. A. (ed.), 'The Bandlet of Righteousness' (Lefefa Sedek), Luzac, London, 1929.

Butler, W., 'Magic, its Ritual Power and Purpose', Aquarian Press, London, 1952.

Butler, W., 'The Magician, his Training and Work', Aquarian Press, London, 1959.

Butler, W., 'Magic and the Qabalah', Aquarian Press, London, 1964.

Campbell, J. (ed.), 'Myths, Dreams and Religion', Dutton, New York, 1970.

Case, P., 'The Tarot', Macoy Publishing Co., New York, 1948.

Case, P., 'The Book of Tokens' (8th edn), The Builders of the Adytum, Los Angeles, 1974.

Casteneda, C., 'The Teachings of Don Juan', University of California Press, Berkeley, 1968; reissued jointly with Simon & Schuster, 1973.

Casteneda, C., 'A Separate Reality', Simon & Schuster, New York, 1971.

Casteneda, C., 'Journey to Ixtlan', Simon & Schuster, New York, 1972.

Casteneda, C., 'Tales of Power', Simon & Schuster, New York, 1974.

Casteneda, C., 'The Second Ring of Power', Simon & Schuster, London, 1976.

Chevalier, G., 'The Sacred Magician', Paladin, London, 1976.

Colquhuon, I., 'Sword of Wisdom', Neville Spearman, London, 1975.

Crowley, A., 'Magick in Theory and Practice', privately published, Paris, 1929; reissued by Castle Books, New York (no date) and Routledge & Kegan Paul, 1973.

Crowley, A., 'The Book of Thoth', Weiser, New York, 1969.

Crowley, A., 'Book Four', Sangreal Foundation, Dallas, 1972.

Crowley, A., 'The Vision and the Voice', Sangreal Foundation, Dallas, 1972.

De Martino, E., 'Magic, Primitive and Modern', Bay Books, Sydney, 1972.

De Mille, R., 'Casteneda's Journey', Capra Press, Sant Barbara, 1976.

De Mille, R., 'The Don Juan Papers', Ross-Erikson, Santa Barbara, 1980.

Deikman, A., Deautomatization and the mystic experience, in C. Tart (ed.), 'Altered States of Consciousness', Wiley, New York, 1969.

Deren, M., 'Divine Horsemen: Voodoo Gods of Haiti', Thames & Hudson, London, 1953.

Drury, N., 'The Path of the Chameleon', Neville Spearman, London, 1973.

Drury, N., 'Don Juan, Mescalito and Modern Magic', Routledge & Kegan Paul, 1978.

Drury, N., 'Inner Visions: Explorations in Magical Consciousness', Routledge & Kegan Paul, London, 1979.

Drury, N. and Skinner, S., 'The Search for Abraxas', Neville Spearman, London, 1972.

Drury, N. and Tillett, G., 'Other Temples, Other Gods', Methuen, Sydney, 1980.

Du Toit, B. M. (ed.), 'Drugs, Rituals and Altered States of Consciousness', A. A. Balkema, Rotterdam, 1977.

Edsman, C. M. (ed.), 'Studies in Shamanism', Almquist & Wiksell, Stockholm, 1967.

Ehrenwald, J., 'The ESP Experience', Basic Books, New York, 1978.

Eliade, M., 'Shamanism', Princeton University Press, 1972.

Elkin, A. P., 'Aboriginal Men of High Degree', (2nd edn), University of Queensland Press, St Lucia, 1977.

Farr, F., 'Egyptian Magic' (including extracts from the Leyden and Bruce papyri), Theosophical Publishing Company, London, 1896.

Fortune, D., 'Applied Magic', Aquarian Press, London, 1962.

Fortune, 'The Mystical Qabalah', Benn, London, 1966.

Fox, O., 'Astral Projection', University Books, New York, 1962.

Freeman, D., Shaman and Incubus, vol. 4, 'Psychoanalytic Study of Society', 1964.

Fry, P. and Long, M., 'Behind the Mechanical Mind', Australian Broadcasting Commission, Sydney, 1977.

Fuller, J., 'The Magical Dilemma of Victor Neuburg', W. H. Allen, London, 1965.

Galin, D., The Two Modes of Consciousness and the Two Halves of the Brain, in P. R. Lee et al., 'Symposium on Consciousness', Penguin, New York, 1977.

Ginsburg, C., 'The Kabbalah', Routledge & Kegan Paul, London, 1956.

Glock, D. and Bellah, R. (eds), 'The New Religious Consciousness', University of California Press, Berkeley, 1976.

Goodman, F., Shaman and priest in Yucatan pentacostalism, in A. Bharati (ed.), 'The Realm of the Extra-Human', Mouton, The Hague, 1976.

Grant, K., 'The Magical Revival', Muller, London, 1972.

Grant, K., 'Aleister Crowley and the Hidden God', Muller, London, 1973.

Grant, K., 'Images and Oracles of Austin Osman Spare', Muller, London, 1975.

Green, C., 'Lucid Dreams', Hamish Hamilton, London, 1968.

Green, C., 'Out of the Body Experiences', Ballantine, New York, 1973.

Grof, S., 'Realms of the Human Unconscious', Dutton, New York, 1976.

Halifax, J., 'Shamanic Voices', Dutton, New York, 1979.

Harner, M., 'The Jivaro', Robert Hale, London, 1972.

Harner, M. (ed.), 'Hallucinogens and Shamanism', Oxford University Press, New York, 1973.

Harner, M., 'The Way of the Shaman', Harper & Row, San Francisco, 1980.

Heffern, R., 'Secrets of the Mind Altering Plants of Mexico', Pyramid, New York, 1974.

Hillman, J., 'Revisioning Psychology', Harper & Row, New York, 1975.

Hitchcock, J. and Jones, R., 'Spirit Possession in the Nepal Himalayas', Aris & Phillips, Warminster, 1975.

Hopper, S., Myth, Dream and Imagination, in J. Campbell (ed.), 'Myths, Dreams and Religion', Dutton, New York, 1970.

Howe, E., 'The Magicians of the Golden Dawn', Routledge & Kegan Paul, 1972.

Hultkrantz, A., Spirit Lodge, a North American shamanistic seance, in C. M. Edsman (ed.), 'Studies in Shamanism', Almquist & Wiksell, Stockholm, 1967.

Jung, C., 'Two Essays on Analytical Psychology', Routledge & Kegan Paul, London, 1953.

Jung, C., 'Man and his Symbols', Dell, New York, 1968.

Kasamatus, A. and Hirai, T., An electroencephalograph study on the Zen meditation (Zazen), in C. Tart (ed.), 'Altered States of Consciousness', Wiley, New York, 1969.

Kiev, A., Spirit possession in Haiti, 'American Journal of Psychology', vol. 118, 1961.

Kiev, A. (ed.), 'Magic, Faith and Healing', Free Press, New York, 1964.

King, F. (ed.), 'Astral Projection, Magic and Alchemy', Neville Spearman, London, 1971.

King, F., 'Ritual Magic in England', Neville Spearman, London, 1971.

King, F. and Skinner, S., 'Techniques of High magic', C. W. Daniel, London, 1976.

Knight, G., 'A Practical Guide to Qabalistic Symbolism', vols 1 and 2, Helios, Cheltenham, 1965.

Kretschmer, W., Meditative techniques in psychotherapy, in C. Tart (ed.), 'Altered States of Consciousness', Wiley, New York, 1969.

La Barre, W., Hallucinogens and the shamanic origins of religion, in P. Furst (ed.), 'Flesh of the Gods', Allen & Unwin, London, 1972.

La Vey, A., 'The Satanic Bible', Avon, New York, 1969.

La Vey, A., 'Satanic Rituals', Avon, New York, 1972.

Larsen, S., 'The Shaman's Doorway', Harper & Row, New York, 1976.

Laurence, R. (ed.), 'The Book of Enoch', Kegan Paul Trench Co., London, 1883.

Lee, P. R. et al., 'Symposium on Consciousness', Penguin, New York, 1977.

Lessa, W. and Vogt, E. (eds), 'Reader in Comparative Religion (3rd edn), Harper & Row, New York, 1972.

Leuba, J. H., 'Psychology of Religious Mysticism', Harcourt Brace, New York, 1929. 1929.

Lévi, E., 'The Key of the Mysteries', Rider, London, 1959.

Lévi-Strauss, C., The Sorcerer and his magic, in J. Middleton, 'Magic, Witchcraft and Curing', The Natural History Press, New York, 1967.

Lévi-Strauss, C., 'The Raw and the Cooked', Harper & Row, New York, 1969.

Lewis, I. M., 'Ecstatic Religion', Penguin, Harmondsworth, 1971.

Lex, B., Altered states of consciousness in northern Iroquoian ritual, in A. Bharati (ed.), 'The Realm of the Extra-Human', Mouton, The Hague, 1976.

Lilly, J., 'The Centre of the Cyclone', Calder & Boyars, London, 1972.

Lilly, J., 'Simulations of God', Bantam, New York, 1975.

MacIntosh, C., 'Eliphas Levi and the French Occult Revival', Rider, London, 1972.

Mathers, S. L., 'The Sacred Magic of Abramelin the Mage', De Laurence, Chicago, 1948.

Mathers, S. L., 'The Kabbalah Unveiled', George Redway, London, 1887; subsequent editions, Routledge & Kegan Paul.

Mead, G. R. (ed.), 'Pistis Sophia', John M. Watkins, London, 1963.

Metraux, A., 'Voodoo in Haiti', Andre Deutsch, London, 1959.

Michael, H. N. (ed.), 'Studies in Siberian Shamanism', University of Toronto Press, 1963.

Nachtigall, H., The cultural historical origin of shamanism, in A. Bharati (ed.), 'The Realm of the Extra-Human', Mouton, The Hague, 1976.

Nadel, S., A study of shamanism in the Nuba mountains, 'Journal of the Royal Anthropological Institute', 76, pp. 25–37.

Noel, D. (ed.), 'Seeing Castaneda', Putnam, New York, 1976.

Nordland, O., Shamanism as an experience of the 'unreal', in C. M. Edsman (ed.), 'Studies of Shamanism', Almquist & Wiksell, Stockholm, 1967.

Oesterreich, T., 'Possession', University Books, New York, 1966.

Ornstein, R., 'The Psychology of Consciousness', Penguin, London & New York, 1977.

Potapov, L., Certain aspects of the study of Siberian shamanism, in J. Hitchcock and R. Jones, 'Spirit Possession in the Nepal Himalayas', Aris & Phillips, Warminster, 1975.

Prince, R., Cocoon work: an interpretation of the concern of contemporary youth with the mystical, in I. Zaretsky and M. Leone (eds), 'Religious Movements in Contemporary America', Princeton University Press, 1974.

Reichel-Dolmatoff, G., The cultural context of an Aboriginal hallucinogen: Banisteriopsis Caapi, in P. Furst (ed.), 'Flesh of the Gods', Allen & Unwin, London, 1972.

Reinhard, J., Shamanism and spirit possession, in J. Hitchcock and R. Jones, 'Spirit Possession in the Nepal Himalayas', Aris & Phillips, Warminster, 1975.

Regardie, I., 'The Art and Meaning of Magic', Helios, Cheltenham, 1964.

Regardie, I., 'The Garden of Pomegranates' (2nd edn), Llewellyn, St Paul, Minnesota, 1970.

Robinson, R. (ed.), 'The Nag Hammadi Library', Harper & Row, San Francisco, 1977.

Roszak, T., 'Unfinished Animal', Harper & Row, New York, 1975.

Roszak, T., Myth, magic and mystery, in P. Fry and M. Long, 'Behind the Mechanical Mind', Australian Broadcasting Commission, Sydney, 1977.

Sargent, W., 'The Mind Possessed', Heinemann, London, 1973; Pan, London, 1976.

Schaya, L., 'The Universal Meaning of the Kabbalah', University Books, New Jersey, 1971.

Scholem, G., 'Major Trends in Jewish Mysticism', Schocken, New York, 1961.

Shirokogoroff, S., 'The Psychomental Complex of the Tungus', Rouledge & Kegan Paul, London, 1935.

Shor, R., Three dimensions of hypnotic depth, in C. Tart (ed.), 'Altered States of Consciousness', Wiley, New York, 1969.

Siegal, R., Hallucinations, 'Scientific American', October 1977.

Siiger, H., Shamanistic ecstasy and supernatural beings, in C. M. Edsman (ed.), 'Studies in Shamanism', Almquist & Wiksell, Stockholm, 1967.

Spare, A., 'The Book of Pleasure', London, 1913; reprinted by Publishing 93, Montreal, 1975.

Spare, A., 'Focus on Life', London, 1921; reprinted by Askin Press, London, 1976.

Steinbrecher, E., 'The Guide Meditation', DOME Foundation, Santa Fe, New Mexico, 1977.

Stone, D., The Human Potential Movement, in C. Glock and R. Bellah (eds), 'The New Religious Consciousness', University of California Press, Berkeley, 1976.

Suzuki, M., The shamanistic element in Taiwanese folk religion, in A. Bharati (ed.), 'The Realm of the Extra-Human', Mouton, The Hague, 1976.

Symonds, J., 'The Great Beast: The Life and Magic of Aleister Crowley', Mayflower, London, 1973.

Symonds, J. and Grant, K. (eds), 'The Magical Record of the Beast 666', Duckworth, London, 1972.

Symonds, J. and Grant, K. (eds), 'The Confessions of Aleister Crowley', Hill & Wang, New York, 1973.

Tart, C. (ed.), 'Altered States of Consciousness', Wiley, New York, 1969.

Tart, C., Introduction to Robert Monroe's 'Journey out of the Body', Doubleday, New York, 1973.

Tart, C., 'States of Consciousness', Dutton, New York, 1975.

Tart, C., Discrete states of consciousness, in P. Lee et al., 'Symposium on Consciousness', Penguin, New York, 1977.

Ten Houten, W. and Kaplan, C., 'Science and its Mirror Image', Harper & Row, New York, 1973.

Truzzi, M., Towards a sociology of the occult: notes on modern witch-craft, in I. Zaretsky and M. Leone (eds), 'Religious Movements in Contemporary America', Princeton University Press, 1974.

Underhill, E., 'Mysticism', Methuen, London, 1912.

Waite, A., 'The Secret Doctrine in Israel', OMTBC, Boston, 1914.

Wallace, A., 'Culture and Personality' (2nd edn), Random House, New York, 1970.

Wasson, R. G., The hallucinogenic fungi of Mexico, in G. M. Weil (ed.), 'The Psychedelic Reader', Citadel Press, New York, 1971.

Wasson, R. G., 'The Road to Eleusis', Harcourt Brace Jovanovich, New York, 1978.

Watkins, M., 'Waking Dreams', Gordon & Breach, New York, 1976.

Weakland, J., Shamans, schizophrenia and scientific unity, 'American Anthropologist', vol. 70, 1968.

Weil, G. M. (ed.), 'The Psychedelic Reader', Citadel Press, New York, 1971.

Whitehead, H., Reasonably fantastic: some perspective on scientology, science fiction and occultism, in I. Zaretsky and M. Leone (eds. 'Religious Movements in Contemporary America', Princeton University Press, 1974.

Whitten, P., 'Being Human Today – Psychological Perspectives', Canfield Press/Harper & Row, San Francisco, 1977.

Wilby, B. (ed.), 'New Dimensions Red Book', Helios, Cheltenham, 1968.

Yeats, W., 'Mythologies', Macmillan, London, 1959.

Zaretsky, I. and Leone, M. (eds), 'Religious Movements in Contemporary America', Princeton University Press, 1974.

Index